Thanks for ... interest
in Autism Tom

CAUGHT BETWEEN TWO WORLDS
(My Autistic Dilemma)

Thomas S. Page

with

comments explanations made by

his professionals and parents

Energy Therapist – Susan Dowling

Speech Therapist – Lauren Kruzshak

Physical Therapist – Michael Nelson

Neuro-Optometric Rehabilitation – Dr. William Padula

Occupational Therapist – Darlene Talavera

and

Mother – Joanna Page

Father – Walter Page

Sister – Sally Sherwood

Published by Words of Understanding
Woodbridge, Connecticut

Printed in the United States of America
First Edition

Graphic Design – Ed Ziobron

ISBN: 0-9727181-0-9

Dedication

I would like to dedicate this book to my
parents and all the people who have believed
and encouraged me to become the person I am.
I hope to grow still more and expand my
many dreams and missions.

— Tom

The Worlds Between

In the vast universe of time,
human beings are created.
All have a place in God's infinite plan.
We each have a mission
and a lifetime to find our way.

We are to help one another
to accomplish our goals.
It is like a mystery to unravel
how we interweave and grope
with the intricacies required.

At the end of our time,
we will be evaluated as to our
accomplishments and maybe come back
to finish God's task,
in another time and place.

Then there are the autistic
caught between the worlds.
We have people trying to help,
most not understanding at all.
They push and they tweak
and make things worse,
sending us into deep despair,
our mission to be doomed evermore.

Then out of the blue
a new path is formed.
New people come to the front
with a most positive plan
to make us like you,
even if that is not what we want.

The ingredient that is missing
is what they leave out,
not what they say or they do.
We are spiritual beings
with energies to spare,
often disorganized, but deep.

Professionals, take heed of what
I am saying:
incorporate God in your plan.
Together we can make sense
and music within.
Share together the knowledge you have.
Bring all the pieces to Him.

This and this alone will bring
our worlds together,
and peace of soul to us all.

— Tom Page 7/30/96

Mom's Introduction:
The Family Background

Perhaps a short introduction to our family before you continue into our son Tom's world might be in order. B.T. (Before Tom), we were considered an average, middle class, conservative, mid-western family. Wally and I met and were married post World War II while attending a teachers college.

We became involved with our professions, Wally coaching and teaching, me an elementary teacher in the public schools in Indiana. We then became proud parents of a baby girl and five years later thought we had a perfect world when our family gained a son.

As happens with most families with persons with autism, we did not have any idea of what was ahead when Tom was diagnosed with this disability at age two-and-a-half. We were devastated at the advice of the professionals, at that time, to place him in an institution and forget his existence. This was during the Bruno Bettleheim era, when it was thought "cold refrigerator mothers" were to blame. Obviously, we did not take their advice. We made the decision to do the best for our son and try to make as normal a life for the four of us as possible. I think we did a pretty good job, considering the circumstances. One of the nicest things our daughter ever said as she went to college was "I never really thought our family was different."

When Tom was twelve we moved to the New Haven, Connecticut, area to secure better services for him. It meant moving away from our families, friends and jobs. Our daughter was entering her senior year in high school. The entire family was consulted and in agreement for this move. It was a year of some turmoil, ups and downs, but nothing we couldn't handle. Tom entered a school, one of the few around that were strictly for autistic. I was hired as a teacher in that school. Wally found a job in nearby Bridgeport, a demotion for him, but we were convinced it was the best for the family. Our daughter adjusted to the situation pretty well, although she returned to Indiana the following year to attend college. At this point, Tom's situation became more challenging.

Tom takes up the story a few years later. We have learned much from his insightful, perceptive, honest thoughts. To outward appearances he was not only autistic but profoundly retarded, low functioning and nearly nonverbal. There were occasions when he would, out of the blue, do something or look intelligent in a way that was beyond his assumed capabilities. We were mildly puzzled. His behavior deteriorated and our lives became more complicated.

His schooling consisted of three years of preschool, five years in a school for trainable retarded, nine years in the school for persons with autism and the rest of his years in adult vocational training programs. He received very little actual academic education.

This is a journey with one person with autism and his involvement with some of the people his life has touched. He puts emphasis on the fact that all these people are unique and their stories would be their own to tell. This book is intended to give some insights into the world of autism from his point of view. People with autism, their families and the people who work with them must find their own individual way. Maybe they can identify with many of the situations and learn something of value. Tom wrote this book with the Facilitated Communication (FC) mode of communication. He did not start to communicate until age 36.

The autistic are people with real potential and real feelings. I feel they should respected and heard.

Dad's Introduction:
What Will Happen to Tom?

Worry! Worry! Worry! I still worry, but when I became sixty my constant worry was Tom is getting stronger and I'll be getting weaker.

Although he had autism with its many problems and was considered mentally retarded, our family did many things together and enjoyed life. It was when something would set him off that he became aggressive and difficult to control. We chose activities according to what kind of day Tom was having.

Then – at age 36 – Tom learned Facilitated Communication (FC) and begin learning to express his desires, feelings, interests and thoughts. Most of all he was able to describe many of his problems and give feedback to professionals, staff and parents. We all began to understand each other better.

Tom, my wife and I and five professionals made a commitment to help him have a new life. All of us were used to commitments, but Tom, although he has autism, was inspirational in his deep commitment to change his life. He still has special problems as you will learn. It is hard to believe that we now share interest in current events, history, music, philosophy, religion, etc. We still worry that it might be taken away.We are now a Mom and Dad with a middle-aged son who participates with us intellectually and physically, whose opinion and viewpoint we seek with anticipation. As you will see, his current problems are addressed with special planning, treatment and his input.

Tom's professional team with introductions and professional backgrounds

*They are listed on the following pages
in the order they joined the team*

Speech Therapist – Lauren Kruzshak

Occupational Therapist – Darlene Talavera

Neuro-Optometric Rehabilitation – Dr. William Padula

Energy Therapist – Susan Dowling

Physical Therapist – Michael Nelson

Lauren Kruzshak
Speech Therapist

When I met Tom, I was not even working in the field of speech pathology. I had worked as a speech pathologist for 12 years then left the profession to do other things for 4 years. Prior to that break, I had always worked with children and adults with severe disabilities: cerebral palsy, individuals who were both deaf and blind, infants and children with multiple disabilities, etc. After my 4 year hiatus, I didn't know whether I wanted to work in the communication field but wanted some work with people with disabilities so I got a job as a program supervisor at an employment center for people with autism. It was there I met Tom who I regarded as a particularly disabled man probably with mental retardation in the severe range. My supervisor at the time had been introduced to facilitated communication and urged me to try with Tom, She told me she saw "something" in Tom and thought it would be interesting to try this new technology with him. He was big, he moved around his environment in explosive bursts that made everyone jump with fright and he could be extremely aggressive. This was, not a project I was looking forward to. In addition, I had no idea what I was doing. We struggled using a paper letterboard and I supported Tom pointing to letters, then words. Despite my doubts, I thought I felt some volitional movement when I provided resistance to his pointing movements with my hand. I also videotaped just so I could see, from a more objective perspective, what we looked like when we were facilitating. It was truly trial and error. Though I felt I was stumbling around in the dark, Tom would sit with me for considerable periods of time and try pointing to letters, copying some words and then spelling words that completed fill-in-the-blank statements. It began to dawn on me that maybe this man was not as retarded as I thought and there was cognitive and linguistic ability inside a physical body that did not work very well. From that point, Tom continued to grow and we all began to realize that here was a man who's autism was primarily a motor difference and a sensory processing disorder but who had a wonderful mind and exciting thoughts to share.

In 1993, 1 left the agency that was providing employment opportunities to Tom and began my own private practice in speech language pathology. At that time also, Tom changed agencies and joined a day program run by his group home organization, which in turn, was run by his parents. I followed Tom to his new day program and provided speech-language consultation services both to him and to other people with autism in Tom's agency as well as other organizations around Connecticut As a result of my work with Tom and others, my skills in facilitation grew. Also, I attended FC support groups, went to conferences, shared information with other professionals and read everything I could. Being involved in such a controversial technology has been quite a roller-coaster ride. Despite all the ups and downs, I truly believe there is a place for FC in the lives of some people.

Darlene F. Talavera

Occupational Therapist

Tom Page and I met through my contact for Occupational Therapy Services with Opportunity House, Inc. in 1996. I had just started my own private practice, after working for 11 years for previous agencies and schools who served children, adolescents and adults with significant physical and cognitive disabilities.

Tom's Mother, Jo, was very interested in learning about the sensory integration framework which was my focus for working with people who happened to be diagnosed with an Autistic Spectrum Disorder.

At that time 1996, viewing people with autism from a sensory perspective was not a common practice. Although, I'm very happy to say today in 2002 this is a framework that is highly accepted within the autism community. In the 6 year journey that Tom, Jo and Wally have shared with me, we have learned a tremendous amount about how sensory processing impacts all of our lives. We have attended workshops and conferences together and have provided in-service training for those employed by Opportunity House related to sensory processing and autism. Tom has influenced how I practice occupational therapy with most of my clients on the autism spectrum. I have strived to follow his lead in his ongoing assessment/ information program and have relayed on the insightful input of my colleagues. Tom;s spirit has taught me true persistence in spite of what seems to be a dilemma – living life with autism.

Darlene F. Talavera OTR/L has worked with clients of all ages in many different settings. For the past 9 years Darlene has been in private practice in New Haven County where she has specialized in developing programs for children, adolescents and adults with Autism Spectrum Disorders. Darlene's passion for understanding sensory processing disorders has lead her to many continuing education courses and workshops as well as lecturing herself on the topic in Connecticut and Rhode Island. She has been a therapist for 16 years.

Dr. William Padula
Neuro-Optometric Rehabilitation

Tom was scheduled for a neuro-optometric rehabilitation examination and was accompanied to the appointment by his parents and speech therapist. When I first met Tom, he was rocking in his chair and appeared to be quite anxious about the new experience. Tom was able to use facilitated communication and reported to me that his family and therapists were working with him to increase his independence. Her told them, "First please get my eyes straightened out."

The visual examination was oriented to Tom. He later explained that he was very surprised I had directed my questions to him instead of his parents or therapist. He told me that because of his disability, doctors rarely spoke directly to him. Instead, they spoke about him to his parents or therapists. He answered my questions the best he could but due to his anxious state, he had moments of verbalization (loud sounds) and had to stand up and walk about the room. Tom's anxiety overtook him and he began banging his head on the wall. Following the examination, I explained Tom's visual difficulties and recommended prism glasses with binasal occlusion.

Tom returned to my office to receive the glasses and appeared to be in a more anxious state than the previous visit. He was quite concerned about the changes that were going to occur from using prism glasses. It was apparent to me that Tom wanted this change, but had a considerable amount of fear about how it would change his life. Upon initially fitting the glasses, it was decided that Tom would use the glasses at his own level of ability. I explained that despite the fact we all had observed positive changes from use of the prism glasses, we needed to develop a respect of Tom's ability to accept this change. Despite our recognition of immediate positive changes, Tom might not be able to accept all these changes immediately. Therefore, Tom became part of the planning for use of these prisms. He was given the opportunity to explain when he could wear them as well as when he needed to remove them.

My initial contact with Tom recognized his extraordinary intellect and use of language through facilitation. Tom's depth of language was amazing. It was also apparent to me that Tom needed a group effort by everyone involved to assist him in achieving his potential.

William V. Padula, O.D.,F.A.A.O., F.N.O.R.

William V. Padula, O.D. is Director of the Padula Institute of Vision in Guilford, Connecticut. He is a graduate of the Pennsylvania College of Optometry and a Fellow of the Neuro-Optometric Rehabilitation Association. Dr. Padula has been a consultant to the National Academy of Sciences Committee on Vision. Dr. Padula has conducted research in discovering Post Trauma Vision Syndrome and Visual Midline Shift Syndrome. He has served as the Director of the Low Vision Clinic at the Rehabilitation Center in New Haven, Connecticut and was a national consultant in Low Vision Services for the for the American Foundation for the Blind and Director of Vision Research to the Gesell Institute of Human Development. He has also consulted and developed a low vision clinic named in his honor at the Zhongshan Eye Research Hospital in Canton, China and regularly consults with the Centro de Aprendizaje de Cuernavaca in Mexico. He is on the staff at the Hospital for Special Care in New Britain, Connecticut and consults with many programs for head-injured persons through out the United States.

Dr. Padula has written numerous publications including a book, *Neuro-Optometric Rehabilitation,* and has developed three award winning professional video tapes about vision, Post Trauma Vision Syndrome, and Visual Midline Shift Syndrome. He has also been awarded four U.S. patents.

Susan Dowling
Energy Therapy

Dr. Padula introduced me to Tom in March 1995. I had been discussing and explaining my practice of energy therapy with Dr. Padula for many months. He urged me to meet Tom as he felt I might be able to connect with Tom from a little different angle than the other practitioners working with him.

When it came time to meet Tom, I could tell by the sound of things on the other side of my colleagues door that this wasn't going to be a familiar encounter for me. Vibrations, sounds and rhythmus in varying degrees played out a repetitive theme as they emanated through the walls. I questioned why I was present, remembering my colleagues urging words "I think you have something to offer him, I think you will understand." Today I now know that it was the gentle man that I was about to meet that would do the offering.

Tom was seated at the end of the room surrounded by his parents and my colleague. His ecolalia song was different than any I had heard before. He rocked softly in his chair, while tapping his hand rhythmically and repeatedly on his thigh. His eyes darted about the room taking in his surroundings. Although I had been told that Tom suffers from autism, having had no previous experience with this population was a blessing in disguise.

I knew that what I was feeling in this moment was a deep compassion and gratitude for the magic of life in all it's form and the unique garb our souls dress our bodies in.

It was difficult to believe that just three years earlier Tom was considered profoundly retarded, low functioning and autistic. Sad labels that had followed him for most of his life. It was not expected that this would change for he was well into his thirties with little improvement. Although this was the outward appearance, it was hardly the case.

When I think about our initial meeting I often equate it with what it must have been like to connect with Helen Keller. If one does not use the usual main sensory system to communicate with, then what? I knew from the start that I needed to connect with Tom in a more unique way.

What I have learned, and I suspect many practitioners understand, is that the way in which we hold our intentions, our emotions, our thoughts, our "energy" has a profound effect on the outcome of our connections in our relationships. This is especially true with those who operate with a sensory system that is unlike that which we might consider "normal" and I have found this to be the missing link to understanding the very nature of these individuals.

Energy therapists are trained to experience the world from a deeply holistic nature. Everything is interconnected and holds a particular pattern and is organized often by invisible fields of energy. Each of these fields of energy relate to each other in some subtle way, just like body parts. We look at how things are interconnected and communicate not only from a tangible, solid material framework but also from the not so visible electromagnetic fields that make up every aspect of life.

Each of us has had the experience of "feeling" that a particular environment in which in where we enter, is either friendly or uncomfortable. This concept is easily understood when we consider the interaction of energy fields.

When energy waves interact they create specific configurations each with unique structures, frequencies and movements. These patterns make up all animate and inanimate objects. The air we breath, the clothing we wear, the thoughts we have, the furniture we sit on, all have vibratory patterns. How we hold and express our own bodily vibrations and how these vibrations interact within our environment creates a particular response.

Using this model of vibrational communication, my initial contact with Tom for the most part was non-verbal. His response was one of immediate recognition and he expressed that this approach helped him feel safe.

Our work together over the years has involved the use of energy treatments on a bimonthly basis. These treatments have included working with Tom's defense system and the subsequent energy field distortions that helped to create his entrapment. Through slow progressive positive contact on all four levels- physical, emotional, mental and spiritual, Tom has learned to trust the integration of these interacting systems. This has contributed to an increased expansion of the layers of the field that were severely constricted allowing a more integrated, flowing, communication of information entering the system. He has moved from a deeply contracted state to a more flexible multi-tasked individualistic state, no longer rooted in a system of fear and inflexibility.

Susan Dowling Cert. HS has worked in the field of human development and the healing arts for twenty years. She holds a four year certification in Healing Science from the Barbara Brennan School of Healing as an energy therapist. She has also practiced as a childbirth educator and for eight years advocated for the needs of victims of domestic violence as a certified battered woman's counselor for the State of Connecticut. Susan has multifaceted training in the human energy field, bioenergetics, intuitive counseling group process, sacred ceremony and shamanic practices in the native traditions. She uses contemplative process and compassion as a way to conscious healing and spiritual awakening. She maintains a private practice in Guilford, Connecticut, where she sees adults and children for energy work and spiritually based holistic healing.

Michael Nelson
Physical Therapist

I first met Tom with a quick glance at Dr. Padula's office in December of 1996. He had been the previous appointment with Dr Christine Nelson to an appointment I had with another client. He walked (or should I say ran) though the waiting room with his father about 10 minutes prior to his Mother and my colleague and friend Darlene Talavera OTR/L. It was a pleasant surprise when I saw Darlene walk into the waiting room with Mrs. Page. She introduced me to Mrs. Page and told me that they had just talked about me in the consult with Dr. Nelson. Everything happens for a reason. This was my first introduction to Tom and his parents. Darlene and Jo Page said that they would be calling me to see if I could be a consultant to Tom's program. I was to be the NDT component that the team was looking for to complete the areas of intervention for Tom.

I have been a practicing Physical Therapist for the past 23 years with 99 percent of my experience in the field of Pediatrics. I worked in a VA Hospital when I first graduated for a brief duration in a temporary position and when it was over I entered the world of Pediatrics. When I say pediatrics I include adults that have had childhood onset of neurological or orthopedic conditions. I have worked in Special Education Schools, Regular Public Schools, an Outpatient Pediatric Clinic, Birth to Three Agencies, Home Care Agencies, Group Homes, Lectured at the College Level and have serviced Private clients in their homes and community settings. I graduated from Quinnipiac College in 1978 and earned my Pediatric NDT Training in 1984.

My clinical and professional interests have been varied and some of the areas of continuing education have been in the areas of Sensory Integration, Biomechanics, Educationally related issues, NDT (basic and advanced levels), and over the past few years I have been expanding my professional journey with Cranial Sacral Therapy courses through the Upledger Institute. This is a partial list of stuff that I have done that contributes to my overall theories of practice. I view myself as an eclectic therapist utilizing each new experience to expand my knowledge and ability to serve the children and adults that I am in contact with. I hope that I have assisted Tom in his journey of advancement, enhancement and development of life skills. I know that he has assisted me in mine.

CONTENTS

LIST OF POEMS

LIST OF THOUGHTS

PHOTOS

This Book was Typed with Facilitated Communication

Facilitated communication is a means of expression that attempts to accommodate a motor difference. In this technology, a facilitator supports a user's hand or arm and backward resistance is given to forward pointing movements. The hand is never lead to the target, which could be pointing to pictures, whole words or phrases, or letters. In Tom's case, support and backward resistance is given to his hand, which enables him to point to letters to construct words on a letter board or on a computer key board.

Facilitated Communication (FC) is a controversial means of communication. It is a hands-on technology and to the naive eye it looks as though the user's hand is being pushed and pulled toward letters or words. In Tom's situation, often observers watching this process think, how can someone who looks so challenged, is capable of such sophistication? A major component of Tom's autism is his motor planning skills. What the facilitator does to help Tom compensate for his motor challenge allows his language competency to be expressed. Those of us who have been facilitating with Tom a long time feel very comfortable with his facilitation. Personally, he has disclosed enough information to me that I did not know, but could verify later, to calm my anxieties about using this technology that is so controversial in my own profession.

Lauren Kruzshak – Speech Therapist

This book was written by Tom with the aid of
two facilitators – Mom and Dad.

Voice with No Noise

My voice is naked.
God has chosen the fabric,
texture and color.

My soul is determining
the pattern
and my fingers are stitching
it together.

May it be a garment
worthy of making
a statement
for mankind.

Tom Page – 2002

PART I
My Reason for Writing This Book

This book is about me. It is not the usual story of the life of a person with autism. It is the story of myself, a person with autism who is relatively nonverbal, with a history of severe violence and how I made significant changes in my life, even though middle aged. These changes in my life came about with the help of several people and commitment and determination on my part and the help of God.

I have had no formal education in writing but I want to show all people, whether they are autistic or not, that they can change their lives, too, if they have the will and the help and inspiration of dedicated others. There is no formula since we are all different with different problems to solve. I hope you can find in this book the ways, means and inspiration that will help you attack life on the terms that you have options and don't have to passively sit by and accept what is passed to you on your plate.

Even though some persons with autism and special needs can read, I hope a caring person will read it with them so they can discuss it. If the person with autism or special needs cannot read, you should read it to them whether you think they understand it or not. They may not appear to be listening, they may not be looking at you, they may be making noise or even walking around. This is not uncommon for our disability. You may feel strange but it will pay off. They will respect you for it. This respect partly comes from love, but the rest comes from how you interact with them. You can love an object and not have to interact with it. People need to understand we are not objects, we are people like you and want this. On the surface we sometimes appear to be fighting you. It is because we are really frightened and scared.

You and your person with autism or special needs, both, must have a great deal of determination and willpower or you won't

1

succeed. This can come from God or your own inner source of power. It is strong desire and will that counts; each of you can energize the other. This must be present in both of you. If it were easy it would be sold over the counter like medicine. Remember, if you truly have the desire God will furnish the help. Phony desire is easy for God to detect. I'm telling you all is possible if you believe and are willing to ask for help and then follow through. The desire must be transferred into work and commitment. God does not do the work, he just makes all things possible. Take charge of your life, it is the only way!

Life CAN Begin at Age Thirty-Six

I am very lucky to be living at this time when the world is taking a new look at the people with special needs. It is a time when people with special needs can catch a ride to more freedom and understanding. I have caught my ride and am making my journey, so world, look out – here I come. It is similar to a line from a favorite song of mine and it tells it like it is.

It is a better way, that more people are using, to treat others with special needs. They are considered people now and treated as such. In this book, I'm going to tell of my struggles and improvements but this will <u>not</u> be another life story. I want this to be a helpful book of my improvements, not a glorification of Tom Page. I am in my early forties, a middle-aged teenager, with high expectations. You will know it is true because I was a 36-year-old blob, with little communication skills, doing nothing of any consequence except taking up space.

It was the miracle of FC that opened the window and let me out in the world. You don't know what a great feeling it was. I felt like soaring to the heavens and back. I felt released from my bondage.

It is not always important for you to know why I did things when I was young, but it is important for you to know the kind of person I had been. It is not the part of my story that I like to tell. I am not proud of many parts of it but I am here now and doing well. **It is to show that it is not too late even for a middle-aged man**. The sun is shining on a new day even if the clouds blocked it for many years. I want to show how the clouds were rolled back and the sun peeked through.

How I had been will tell you why I was in trouble most of my life. The trouble was not of my choosing but how I perceived the world around me and the world perceived me. It is a good thing that I couldn't control my environment to my own choosing. This would have made me a happy soul, but completely dysfunctional. Having your environment exactly to your liking won't solve further problems.

It will only delay them. The solution must be found as soon as possible because one problem brings on another, like the domino effect that the scientists and people love to talk about. It is a normal thing to try to get what you want. People with autism cause trouble to a greater degree because their problems are more severe. It would not be a good thing that we be given a world that fits us completely or it would be our holding pen the rest of our lives. Having patience but a mutual goal is the answer. <u>The big question is what adjustments can we make and what should the world accept.</u> <u>The answer will lead us into the light of day.</u>

(Dad This is a very difficult question to answer. All persons with autism are different. Most need some adjustments. Some of the ones with severe problems need major adjustments to survive in this world. After Tom had made his commitment for improvement and we were able to communicate with him, it became easier for us. We can plan with him and get his feed back on how things are working. Every small improvement makes another possible.)

In my case, when I did many things, oftentimes I couldn't get it together. My senses and body parts didn't work as a unit. My real problems were not known at that time, and the world would not adjust to me. It tried to make me fit into whatever was available at the time. We did not have a chance to ask for anything that would help us in our pain, but instead were told we must be like those who are not autistic.

It is a very hurtful feeling to think you are subhuman in the eyes of most people, but that is how I felt. It was especially hurtful when nearly all professionals that I came in contact with did not consider my feelings as much as their prestige when discussing my problems and future. It may have been out of ignorance or fear of failure. They talked about me in my presence like I wasn't even there. In this way they never considered me as a person. It was not under my control to show them anything else. They had their scales of "humanness" and when they held me up to it, their verdict was "guilty as charged." They never looked for underlying things that would show my individual humanness. I was held to their diagnostic standards. In this way I could fit into their programs or studies. It was a very humiliating process to go through.

4

I did not have sophisticated thinking in those days, but I had sophisticated feelings!

To take it a step further, you **must** fit their programs or studies. If they did not have one for you, most didn't try to make one like they should but tried to push hard to make you fit. You were the proverbial square peg in a round hole. I never adjusted! It was a miserable feeling of pain and failure all the time.

Professionals, parents and persons with disabilities many times fought each other tooth and toenail for control of all situations. It is a real joy to see the beginnings of cooperation in working with each other. The next generation to fight autism is now at hand and you should know that you are a jump ahead of my generation.

I get up each day now knowing that I will have an opportunity to make suggestions in my life. It is like living in a different world. I'm not the enemy anymore but a person with feelings like the rest of the world. Most of the time I have it within my power to make choices and decisions and explain myself to others who have the job of working with me. **They may not always be able to help me but we understand one another and can work towards a common goal**. It is this that brings about progress. It is a new day! Let's rejoice, for now we are heading for heaven on earth together!

PART 2
Me, Before My New Life

Early Life

In the beginning of my life I was a frightened little boy. The world was very confusing because my senses didn't work right. The people that loved me took it pretty good. I had all the love and care that any child had and more. People were puzzled at my behavior but most accepted it because they understood that my parents were doing their best.

They said I was an attractive child and were very proud of my looks. I also could do some things that others couldn't do. My physical ability seemed to be intact. It was when my senses were involved I fell apart. Now I understand the problem but at that time it seemed like a bad dream. I was like a boy who had the physical ability but couldn't use it right because he kept receiving mixed messages.

The world wasn't consistent; it was always sending back those mixed messages so I never knew what to expect. I hear people and staff always saying you've got to be consistent and they are right. If I hadn't had parents who tried to do this, I'm sure it would have been unlimited chaos for me.

In the long run we assembled a life that was functional. I will always remember the good times and regret my bad ones. It was a family that stuck together and worked out strategies to cope. I had a loving sister who was five years older than me. She was disappointed in me but still loved me as a good sister would. We have good memories of our childhood together, but there are some things I would like to forget. Many times I was given an opportunity to mix with her friends. I really appreciated the opportunities and sometimes it worked and sometimes it didn't, but when it didn't they tried to do their best.

I am telling you this because I want you to know my life had many happy moments. As I listen to the many stories the people with autism tell, they stress the bad things they went through. They do this so that the public will understand our problems. I will drop the shoe too, but first let's hear a cheer for all who have put up with us. They have the scars to prove it but they also have had many good laughs, and when we accomplished things, it was a thrill to them too. It is this camaraderie that makes our world go round.

My first major point: you don't always see what you get. We may not look at you and make that wonderful eye contact, we may not smile at the right time, we may even strike you when you don't know why, but we love you. It is the ones that stick with us that deserve more than we can give. It is like new neighbors that are hard to get to know. Some may be frightened of the new neighborhood because they don't feel worthy and are afraid to make overtures. Meet them more than halfway and help them overcome their fright and faults and you may have the truest friends you ever knew.

It is the same with us, we need the extra mile that many give. I will cover my faults and I know that the extra mile has many barriers to overcome. It may be a unifying detour along the way that does the trick. It will be an interesting journey. It is important you know that I had real problems that were difficult to handle. In many cases I became violent and the older I got the more dangerous I became. Times that were really bad were the ones involving my mother when my Dad was not there. It was especially dangerous when she was transporting me in the car. She never wavered, she took me to school every day regardless of her fright. I would attack her while she was driving but it was seldom. She would pull over and work hard to get me under control. It happened often enough to make all our trips to school scary ones. In the house I would throw tantrums that lasted sometimes into hours. As I got older it got louder and more violent. It was fortunate that my Dad was a school teacher and came home near the time I did. Not often but sometimes we would have quite a tussle. It was a fight with no winners. I really was the winner because they stuck with me. In the long run, especially my Mom could sense my moods and problems, so many things were averted. By the way, the women in the family could handle themselves physically. Sometimes they ganged up on me and sometimes it was a tag-team event.

(*Mom – Violence had never been a part of either Wally's or my family's lives. As Tom has said, it didn't suddenly come out of the blue. It was always there, but many children strike out – just doesn't hurt much. The difference was:*

1) We didn't understand why it happened;

2) The traditional methods of dealing with it had no effect. As Tom got older, it hurt and he learned new violent methods of hitting, etc.

It should be noted that Tom has never been on behaviorial altering medication. We came very close a few times, but opted not to at the last minute. I am not advocating this approach. Don't even know if it was a wise decision. He has had valium a few times but I am not sure if it was very effective.)

Going out in public was the best part of my day. I wanted to mix with the world but it was chancy. We went many places if my behavior was good. If my behavior interfered with others I would be taken out. I know what the outside of many places look like. Parking lots are my specialty. It was this way most places we went. Our plan worked for us and that is what most families need.

I hope you don't have the impression that I did not have a good life when I was young. My family was determined my sister would have a normal life in spite of me. They always had a plan when we went places. My Mom and Dad took turns taking me out when my behavior was interfering with others. Noise was the major problem. It caused my exit most of the time. It was impossible for me to control. So, what kind of day I was having decided my part of the agenda.

Please note that we did our best to function like a family. We all feel we did a good job of that. We all feel loved by one another. It may be those sacrifices on all sides that created the bond.

As I got older the screaming was still there and I could hit harder. What was a nuisance before became a danger. What had been a fly became a mosquito, then a lion, until I was an 6' 2" elephant that weighed over 200 pounds. When I got mad people became frightened of me. Fortunately, I never hurt anyone permanently, but my blows did hurt.

Part of my problem was communication. It was frustrating to want something or want to stop something that was bothering me and have no way of letting anyone know. It is like the baby who wants to sleep and they shove a bottle in its mouth or it wants to be picked up and Mother lays it down. The baby cries and flails and no one is in big trouble. If a 6' 2" elephant is frustrated you better look out. It wasn't a problem most of the time. Thank goodness I had some control or could retreat into my autistic world.

During my adolescence was the worst time for my hitting. I still carry the reputation with people that don't know me now. To make it as safe as possible, especially when we went places, my Dad made me a pair of handcuffs. They weren't used often but when they were needed it was good to have them. I had a pair made especially for me. They were made of webbing and velcro so they would not hurt. I could have pulled them off if I wanted to. They were used to protect others when I became aggressive. It would allow my parents to get me to a safe place and cool down. They were used discreetly and only a couple of times where others could see. They would get them out and I would even stop and allow my parents to put them on me. I would allow it because I wanted and needed control even though I would still try fighting after they were on.

It is not my wish to strike people, but I could not control myself. I want a method of control to help me instead of making it worse. It is when I am being held by people that I get infuriated. It is best to make it as impersonal as possible. Shouting and intimidations don't work. If you must hold me, do it quietly and as impersonally as possible. It is a tough world we live in and I'm grateful to the people that were not afraid of me and held me in this manner. The sorry ones that treated me with revenge, I have no sympathy for. They should not be allowed near me. I think this the way most of my aggressive acquaintances with autism feel.

It is important that I tell you about my Dad hitting me back when I got older. He was desperate and afraid that if I didn't get under control, someday I would be in a locked ward. He decided to hit me back hard, so I would know what it felt like and would stop. It only made matters worse. After it was obvious it didn't work, he gave up and just held me down. The difference between his hitting and hitting with revenge is attitude. It sounds funny but I can tell whether you are doing it for me or for revenge. This is one of the first things Dad and I talked about when we could FC together. It made us both feel better to get it off our chest. I tell you this story so others may learn and reconcile differences. We would do anything for one another. We were never really mad or hateful over the fights but just discouraged. It was a necessary evil we both endured. To talk about it relieved our minds. It is one thing to hate and another to be temporarily hateful, but you still want it to be resolved.

(*Dad – I'm glad Tom put this in. What he says is true. I was very glad we could talk it out. I think we are closer than ever now. Even before we could communicate with FC, we could read in one another's eyes remorse and forgiveness after there was an incident.*)

The Two Me's

Life has been for me
confusing as can be.
I never know from when
which Tom will descend.

At times he is so peaceful.
At times he is at war.
I want the peace so bad
and the war nevermore.

I wish I could control
the rage that seeks inside,
It feels so bad to see the hurt
that is there when it subsides.

I try and try to do my best
and hope I may succeed
to find the elusive magic key
and unlock the control I need.

Vision

People that knew me in the past would be surprised to know that vision was one of my worst problems. It still is. If you don't look at something people think you are not interested. If you really look the other way they think you are not normal. It is a problem that most people with autism have dealt with all of their lives. Most people have abnormalities and others overlook them when they understand. It is hard to overlook some of ours but give us a break. I use peripheral vision, photographic memory or other means and can see well enough but not good. I do this because my eyes will not hold their focus. When I try to look closer at things the image breaks up. As long as I am relaxed, I can walk around glancing at things and my vision appears to be normal. I hope you will read what Dr. Padula has to say about it. He is a very perceptive man and understands how I tick. The problem of not looking at things seems to be hard for some people to grasp. They are told about it but still treat me as though I am uninterested or not even aware. I don't mean to insult them, but they are the ones who are not aware. They don't even bother to try to work with me under those conditions. I think they are afraid to look strange, or it could be they just don't get it. It is a sorry person who can't take a chance, but it is how I learn and some won't give me the chance. In this environment I remained most of my life. It has only been the last few years that the understanding is taking hold. It has been a long journey but it is nearing the station (airport for you young people). It is gratifying to see my staff that are getting the picture. Where I live I have a lot of good people working with me, but this was a major hurdle for all of them. Remember! I may not be looking at you or it, but I am interested and caring. The vision may not be good, but I am smarter than you think. I have been accommodating all my life. Give **me** your undivided attention.

(Dr. Padula – When I first met Tom, his parents had brought him to me for neuro-optometric rehabilitation examination. Tom was quite apprehensive at the time of the first visit. I could tell he was aware of what I was saying. He demonstrated little regard for me directly. It was my impression, however, that he was attending to everything I said and all that was occurring about him without giving signs of direct visual attention. This is not uncommon for persons with autism. As Tom has described in his book, he has considerable difficulty in organizing how to look centrally at someone or something. This can cause a major social challenge in our society. While we take it for granted, our social culture has developed around our ability to use vision and make contact with other people. Attention is often perceived by others to be related to how well the person develops fixation and eye contact.

In Tom's case, we might as well have asked him to climb Mt. Everest all by himself and without oxygen. To develop central fixation and deal with the visual problems that he had were insurmountable.

The examination enabled me to understand that Tom had considerable difficulty with organizing the spatial framework in his visual process. Let me begin by explaining briefly about the processing centers in the brain for vision.

Seventy percent of all sensory nerves in the entire body come from the two eyes. It has been said that over eighty percent of all learning occurs through a child's vision. We take for granted this significant process and all that must be done through vision to facilitate learning and development of a child.

The visual process is really composed of at least two separate processing centers. Most people think that vision occurs only in one area, the occipital cortex, which is where the image is established. It is interesting to note that of the 1,900,000 nerve fibers that exit the eyes, 20 percent of these send information down to the midbrain in order to match up information with balance and movement centers. This is part of the visual process that a child first experiences immediately after birth. The child uses this portion of the visual to gain spatial information for the purpose of posture, movement and anticipation of change. This process has been called the ambient visual process. Once information is established with other sensory motor systems, a feedforward mechanism delivers this information to the higher seeing part of the brain. The higher seeing part of the brain has been called the focal process. The reason for this is that this portion of the brain locks into detail. If all we had was the focal process, then we would only see the world as a mosaic of detail and have a very difficult time putting relationships together from one piece to the other.

In Tom's situation, he lacked the ability to spatially organize the details together to form whole relationships. In a severe state of visual fragmentation, a person would have difficulty looking at the face of someone else and being able to recognize who that person is because all they would see would be details of an eye, nose, lip, shadows and lines. It is the ambient process that brings balance to the focal system. It helps the focal system release from the detail and organize itself so that it can establish spatial relationships between the detail. In turn, one can recognize a person's face not by the detail, but by the relationship of the details. At the time of the first examination, I determined that Tom was suffering from over-focalization. In my research, I have called this post trauma vision syndrome. I recommended that Tom wear glasses with a low amount of prism and binasal occlusion to help establish structure and function in the ambient process. Binasal occlusion are vertical lines on the nasal portion of each lens. The reason for this is that the ambient visual process does not see detail, but pays attention to vertical and horizontal boundaries in our environment. The binasal occlusion assists the ambient visual process in restructuring or organizing itself in relationship to the sensory motor system.

Tom began using the glasses. Within a short period of time, he was able to respond through facilitated communication that his vision felt more balanced and he was able to begin to establish central fixation for short periods of time before his vision began to fragment again.

Tom also had another phenomena produced by the same visual processing problem. I have called this visual midline shift syndrome. The ambient visual process is also responsible for helping a person determine where the center of his or her body is. When there is a misjudgment to the visual system, the ambient visual process will shift the concept of where it thinks the center of the body is. In turn, it produces a spatial distortion, and it is as if the brain is perceiving the floor as being tilted in one direction or the other. In Tom's case, he demonstrated a visual midline shift syndrome. The prism in the glasses was designed to affect this condition. It was observed very quickly that when Tom utilized the prisms, he did not lean forward and scuff his feet on the floor but instead stood more erect and had a longer stride with heel contact.

While Tom had made the decision to move ahead with visual rehabilitation, he was quite apprehensive about this and it produced much anxiety for him. It is important that when recognizing visual problems, as well as any other type of physical or psychological problem, respect the individual's ability to make change. Although we as professionals and laymen see positive results often from rehabilitation, it is difficult for us to understand why a person may not want to wear glasses full time or have an increased number of physical or occupational therapy sessions because positive changes have occurred after just a few sessions. Persons who are autistic can accept change but sometimes only on a limited time schedule. It is important for us as professionals and laymen to respect an autistic person's ability to make change. To attempt to push or rush the process will only cause more frustration , anxiety and eventual failure as opposed to success. I discussed this with Tom, as well as with the professionals who were working with him. We agreed that Tom should have the option to be able to take the glasses off and explain why he needs to take the glasses off. This helped the professionals who were working with him understand Tom in a better way and also assist them in adapting the neuro-optometric rehabilitation program to Tom.

Movement Difficulties

In the beginning I had no way to guide my motor skills; it was instinct that led the way. I soon could do many physical skills but as I got older they became more difficult. It is a shame I could not be frozen in time, because I was able to fulfill most of my physical desires at that period of life. It seemed like it was the special instructions and special needs, that were not part of the natural environment that threw me. I know now that my physical ability was there, but my guidance system wasn't working right and my takeoffs and landings were not only terrible – so were the rest of my initiatives. In other words, if I were an airplane I could fly well but not to special destinations. My sensory motor system was not giving good information to the brain. I could imitate pretty well and do things that came naturally or had a high motivating factor. I could react well to other's action such as catching a ball but could not throw it without being given a command with prompts. In the things I did well you will see that desire played a big part and I was able to do things that many others couldn't do. The best example is learning to swim. I was about three and we went to the pool most days that summer. They had a shallow place but I did not want to play there. I wanted to be in the big pool with the other people. Since I couldn't swim my folks took turns holding me. I would struggle to get loose until they finally let go of me. Of course I sank but still struggled to stay afloat. One day I was struggling and my feet came up and I was swimming on my back. Everyone was surprised including me. I wasn't ready for the Olympics, they didn't have a name for my stroke, but I became seaworthy and water became my world. I didn't have proper methods but got many things done. You may not need another example of lack of initiative but it is my story and I'm especially proud of this accomplishment: When I was about six I would walk out to the end of the high board pulling my sister behind me. She did not know why. My Mother did and told her to push me off. It was great, it was what I wanted. From then on, we spent a lot of time doing it together. It was a very long time before I knew I could jump off without her. Again, I want to say, my Mother has great intuition, she knew my thoughts. We went to the ocean most summers for one week each year. I learned to negotiate waves early with my own methods. I think people with autism could adopt the song, "I Did It My Way."

Next, I loved playgrounds and any contraption was fair game. The swing was my favorite it gave me peace and a sense of well-being. Now that I look back, I think when I was in the swing, things would whiz by so fast that they didn't have time to register on my sensory system. It gave me a sense of euphoria. My folks took me often and we had a lot of happy hours there. Again it is appropriate that I thank my sister, she made it a great experience too. If you are a sibling, remember, we don't have natural social graces and you will seldom be thanked with a word but it will be with the heart. We had a nice swing set for the back yard. I was able to walk across the top of it with out holding on to anything. I was not afraid and completely confident. This seemed to make it work. I often wonder if I had the same attitude about talking would the words come out? I loved to swing on my trapeze and had natural body motion to keep going. I had a tether ball and could swing around it like a Maypole but didn't like to play on it as my sister did. I didn't have much trouble throwing and catching balls of all kinds but since I couldn't initiate the throw and other things, my interest in using them has not developed much. An example: My Dad wanted me to learn to shoot a basketball. When we went to the gym by ourselves he would ask me to shoot at the basket, which I had no desire to do. He would bribe me by allowing me to swing out over the floor on a climbing rope. Artificial motivation but it worked. I can still shoot pretty good but can't use it. It is the same now, I have big initiation problems. Ping pong and volley ball worked pretty good but I couldn't move my feet to get the balls back if they weren't reasonably close. This is a problem I may bring up to my P.T., Mike Nelson. Forties is not too late. It is also true that motor planning plays an important part in the vocational field. I was no star there either, it was torture when they ask me to do something. I can remember when I was about twelve or thirteen years old, they would tie us together so we would be aware of one another when asked to go through a maze of objects, to complete a task together, or do any task. They were right; we weren't aware of one another, but we did not understand what we were trying to accomplish. I'm sure they tried to explain it but that old communication bug reared its ugly head. In those days we had great difficulty working with one another. I was totally confused when I had to do a task with one or two people. We were asked one day to go get two walking boards. There were two of us and two boards. The two boards were close to one another and my partner and I each picked up an end. The only problem, it was not the same board we picked up. We both stood there not knowing what to do, each was right and each was wrong. We then pulled them around. I was embarrassed but couldn't solve my problem. To make matters worse, it was a story told over and over about us. It taught other staff to be aware of our problems but no one bothered to assure us that we did nothing wrong and just needed to be straightened out. Like many teachers , even the good ones in those days, they talked about us, laughed about us, and unwittingly set us back a long way in our self-esteem. At this time, I really needed understanding and sensitive teachers because I was failing and sinking fast. Dan was the teacher that sent us on the task that we bungled and told the story the first time. It is here I want to say that he was very sensitive to our needs and was one of my lifesavers. I had some who kept me afloat, and others that unknowingly were pushing me down. Most of them were good people trying to do their job, but it is the ones that are really not into us that do the damage. It is a miracle God sends us the lifesavers.

Tactile

In the beginning of life I must not have needed my senses as much or they did not develop as they should until later. You know that because I walked on time and did most things right. It was after I started to grow, things began to show up that caused problems. I had little feeling in much of my body but could get by anyway. An example – when I was very small I would escape from the house and my Mom would find me out in the snow in my bare feet. I don't remember them feeling cold, but Mom would be very upset. Also, she tried to make me wear socks and slippers in the house; I would take them off, too. The problem was that you can't learn without proper feeling or touch. It is a very important part of learning. The other senses depend on them for guidance. You cannot function well without reliable feedback from them. It is like a fish in water and no tail fin to guide it. It was those early years I needed an occupational therapist. People don't know you have poor touch unless there is an accident or special need that makes it obvious. It is apparent that you might have problems but not be able to pinpoint them. My hands have the feeling of touch but little else. I can catch things and throw things so everyone thinks my hands are OK. They need to watch me feel clothing; there is little sensation. I know it feels good because it is told to me. I know it looks good because I can take a picture in my mind. A quality touch is not there. I touch my horse and there is little feeling of the coat he has. I feel good vibrations from him but no warmth or good feeling when I stroke his neck. The things I feel have little life to me. Oh, to be a Helen Keller and get so much love and information from a touch. The next thing I remember about feelings is my wearing boots when it was cold outside. My mother said the water from the melting snow would get in my boots and I never seemed to notice. The only thing I remember, it was fun. The one thing I always remember was the feeling of water. I loved to play with the lawn hose. I would squirt it up in the air and let the water fall down on me. It really felt good. I also let the waves break against my body when we went to the ocean. Now I know it was tactile touch that I craved. A jump off of the high board really felt great. I think I even threw gravel in the air to feel it hit me when it fell. The playing with ping pong balls and marbles also gave me that quality touch feeling. Only you yourself know that it is a need that is being craved on all parts of the body. You cope with this kind of knowledge but it doesn't solve the problem. You must keep in mind it is not a complete lack of touch that I had but a lack of quality touch. If it had been a complete lack of touch it would have been obvious, and I would have been treated differently. It is like the mother trying to toilet train a child, they treat it differently if it is obvious the child doesn't understand the process. It takes a sensitive mother to make it a smooth process.

I remember my own toilet problems. I would go in the tub when taking a bath but didn't understand it was supposed to be in the toilet. Of course it was exasperating for my folks who would clean it out and start all over again. Again I want to give three cheers for the parents of persons with autism for their patience and persistence even when they are not reading us properly. That is why so many of us survived and had a reasonably good life. I was in the tub one day and they saw I was about to have a bowel movement and flew into action. It had just started and I couldn't stop it as I was wisked through the air from the tub to the toilet. The majority of it went into the toilet and it was claimed to be a howling success. Independence Day did not receive as much enthusiasm as Tom Page did on his liberation day. All the hours of sitting on the toilet and listening to those instructions became a thing of the past. Even those demonstrations didn't work. It was either the wild use of the hand over hand method (sometimes called the "put them through it" method) or pure luck but it was a big change in my life!

Hearing

It was my hearing that caused the most trouble when I was little. Now, something adjusted in my body so that it doesn't bother me much anymore. It was a terrible screeching noise that came and went all the time. It seemed worse at night when everyone else was asleep. I don't know if it caused me to be awake or came after I was awake. Either way, I was not able to sleep much after it hit me. It was so annoying that it kept me awake. It was worse at my Grandparents' house because of the electrical heat in the ceiling. It was a pulsating sound that was there in the winter and not in the summer. It is now, since my understanding is better and the pieces are coming together that I realize what it was. In the years that have followed, my hearing problem is more comfortable and I don't have those screeching sounds anymore. It was those early years that were hellish. It didn't happen often in the day time, but the nights were living hell. Only now do I realize it was not normal. I thought it was part of living. In the daytime, when it was calm, I was OK, but if the wind was blowing, the screeching begain again. It is my hearing that makes it possible to hear sounds that others don't hear. It is a gift now but I earned it the hard way. I can hear both parts of a phone conversation with ease. It is no problem hearing what others are saying in other parts of the house. It is a two-edged sword because you are hurt many times by what you should not hear, but also you hear nice things that are said and not just because you are listening. In the end it has been more of a blessing than a curse. I pray to God everyday and thank him for my gifts. I have a thought I wrote about taking the body that you were given and running with it, you may be surprised at what it can do (see page 24). Let's not sit and let the train pass us by, but get on the platform and be ready for it. The world is ours to have. The person who is willing to do his part will receive his reward in heaven

(Dr. Padula – Tom has done an excellent job at describing his ability to hear fine details that most of us do not. It is interesting to note that he describes his listening ability in a very similar way to what he experiences with his visual process. Tom experiences visual fragmentation due to over-focalization. The same occurrences seem to happen with his hearing. He has an inability to mask out extraneous information. A busy environment with many sounds and voices are as disturbing to Tom as the visual environment of a supermarket at 5:00 p.m. or a shopping mall during the holiday season.)

Energy

I felt disconnected most of my life and didn't know I was different. I just thought everybody felt the same as I had no reference point. Since the beginning of life, I had never felt whole. It is hard to describe but I felt disconnected. It was like part of my body was going one way and another part was doing something else.

I wish to mention one of my therapies at this time. It is energy therapy. It may be new and unusual to most of you and controversial to some. I want to assure you it was one of the best things that happened to me outside of FC. I want to stress the importance of it to me. Keep in mind that it is the team that is important not the individual players. Each segment of my therapies has its own unique place. I want to emphasize energy because it is not usually part of a support plan. It provides the glue and the spiritual aspect that keeps me going.

Energy was easy for me to understand as I think I had always used it in some form. I didn't have the words or organization down but it didn't take me long to pick up what it was all about. I didn't understand its healing power before.

What Sue offered was a new experience for me. I was not expecting what I got. It was a feeling I never had before. The feeling was very pleasurable and made me feel very light like air. After a few sessions I had the feeling of being more connected and whole. However, it didn't last very long but I had a taste of that feeling. It needed reinforcement from time to time. It isn't until recently that it lasts for a much longer period. I look forward to these reinforcement sessions very much. For me it is a very spiritual experience. It seems to help me bring my natural spiritual being into focus. That is very important to me.

My mission in life as well as my determination to meet it have become clearer as a result of Sue's work. It was this therapy that provided the glue for my progress. More about this in my book.

(Sue – For, Tom, and I suspect many autistic, their experience of and response to reality expands way beyond the five senses. As five-sensory humans, the physical body becomes the definition of who we are, an instrument that best allows us to perceive physical reality, and interact within our environment. As multi-sensory beings we are extending our perceptions beyond the physical to capture the intricate interplay of all forms of multi-dimensional existence.

Tom has expressed that he experiences this interplay of multi-dimensional reality as a kaleidoscope of sensory information. He describes the ability to see things from an energetic viewpoint, on the molecular level, always pulsating and changing. One moment an object can appear intact and whole, the next a resonating, vibrating bunch of atoms!

Each of these realities including the physical has a vibratory rate of their own. Our successful interaction with these other realities depends on the extent to which we have developed our body or instrument to respond to the frequency span of each reality.

Although all of these realities exist simultaneously and interconnect, each of us has the task of processing and integrating the incoming information into our own system based on our particular vantage point. Using the energy fields that surround and interpenetrate the physical body, we precipitate energy consciousness from higher realities down into the denser energy forms of the physical, transferring information into our system from the greater universal life force energy field.

Energetically, Tom has not fully entered into the physical body and much of his reality exists on planes other than the physical, ones of a higher vibratory rate. Just as we are expanding our understanding of realities beyond the physical, becoming multi-sensory beings and working to adjust our bodies to accommodate these energy forms; so is this true for Tom as he moves his consciousness from a multi-sensory energy based reality to a more solid physical based reality, accommodating the vibration of the physical plane.)

Early Messages

I was influenced by my family without them being aware. They were active in the church and it was part of their life. I observed them and felt their prayers. It is important to know it is actions more than real words that convey meaning. Never underestimate the power of showing the way. I felt many things besides the religious message. Showing is the best way but words can enhance anything you are trying to get across. I know because I listened to the words spoken around me even though I couldn't speak back. The message had special meaning because it wasn't directed at me with a special purpose. I am telling you this now because it made me more receptive when I was given help from God. You will see what I mean later. Remember we are all constantly sending messages.

PART 3
How My Life Changed

FC (Facilitated Communication) is my main mode of communication. It is a controversial method of communicating that I know is valid. It is built upon trust within our family and others because its authenticity has been demonstrated many times in our lives and interactions. The test of time has proven its worth with me. In the rest of the book facilitated communication shall be referred to as FC.

(Laurie – Facilitated communication is a means of expression that attempts to accommodate a motor difference. In this technology, a facilitator supports a user's hand or arm and provides backward resistance to forward pointing movements. The hand is never lead to the target, which could be pointing to pictures, whole words or phrases or letters. In Tom's case, support and backward resistance is given to his hand, which enables him to point to letters to construct words on a letter board or on a computer keyboard.

Facilitated Communication (FC) is a controversial means of communication. It is a hands-on technology and to the naive eye it looks as though the user's hand is being pushed and pulled toward letters or words. In Tom's situation, often observers watching this process think, how can someone who looks so challenged be capable of such sophistication? A major component of Tom's autism is his motor planning skills. What the facilitator does to help Tom compensate for his motor challenge allows his language competency to be expressed. Those of us who have been facilitating with Tom a long time feel very comfortable with his facilitation. Personally, he has disclosed enough information to me that I did not know, but could verify later, to calm my anxieties about using this technology that is so controversial in my own profession.)

As I progressed with FC I changed my attitude. It is expressed in many thoughts that I write. Below is an example of one.

The Body and Mind May Not Be Perfect,
But Take Them and Run

Never use a lame excuse when you still have a body
and mind that work. It is our responsibility to exercise our
body and mind to help cope with the every-day tasks and
temptations. God gave us a body and mind to work out our
problems. Don't blame him for our shortcomings even
when the body and mind aren't perfect. Take what he has
given us and make it work. Ask for his guidance and you
will be on your way.

— Starting FC —
I Almost Failed FC

The first glimpse I saw of FC was at the adult workplace where
I had been for over 15 years. I was on my way to the bathroom and
I saw a co-worker sitting at a computer in a small room with the
door partially closed. For all I knew, he was being punished for
something, which went on all the time in those days. Isolation was
one of the favorite methods then. At least it helped keep everyone
safe even though it didn't solve any problems.

All that day people seemed to be excited about something. I could
hear in the background that he had done something unexpected. It
must have been good as they were praising him and acting like he
was something special. That is all I remember as it had little meaning
for me. I continued to attempt to make and unmake campaign buttons
as I had been doing for the past 15 years in the workplace. I had no
idea why they had me doing such a stupid thing. My motivation was
zero and my movement difficulties, coupled with my visual problems
made it virtually impossible anyway. I was a prisoner in my chair. At
first I couldn't get out of it and then I was afraid to leave it because
it became my comfort zone. This caused me more trouble than you
can imagine. No one understood my problem; they thought I was
just stubborn or dumb. They were afraid to push me as I displayed
such behaviors that could be very frightening, and they just let well

24

enough alone. It had become worse over the years and I was simply left alone with only prompts to keep me going on those stupid buttons.

Every day someone else would disappear into that mysterious room. When they came out, the staff would grade them with their talk. Either they had told them something funny, or not much or told some family secret, which the staff speculated or analyzed to the hilt. The rest of us sat by and wondered what was going on. The normal people had no idea we understood and they talked and hurt all the time. You have no idea what it feels like to be considered a non-entity.

I was not considered to be a prime candidate and therefore was not a front line prospect. A woman named Mary seemed to have the most success and gained a reputation among the rest of the staff. She was either thumbed up or down, depending on the staff members belief or disbelief of the process. She was called the "Queen of the Facilitators." This term was used as complimentary or derogatory depending on the staff's attitude. They didn't know we were observers and aware of what was going on. A few of the other staff began to try it on their own.

At this time, Laurie, part of my new team, was working at this workplace. She was a speech pathologist herself. Therefore, she was a chief observer. She was never one of the blabbermouths that hurt our feelings. I'm not sure how she got assigned to me when it came my turn to be scrutinized. I'll never forget how scared I was the first time I sat in front of that machine (computer). Failure was in capital letters in my mind. I had no idea what was expected of me, and I just wanted to escape. She gave me directions, I'm sure, but I was too frightened to have remembered what she said. I think she was frightened too. I was considered unpredictable in those days. The first few times were total disasters. She would ask me questions and I was too frightened to respond, and she was too nervous to get it even if I came close. Finally, after quite a few failing sessions, we resorted to as simple a question as possible. I think it was, "Can you spell blue?" I think I came close and we were both happy. This went on for quite a while. We even made a video to show my parents and they were thrilled. It was pretty pathetic by my present standards, but it was a start.

(Laurie – Tom's recollections are quite correct. Our first FC sessions were very anxiety provoking for both of us. I was trying to learn a new means of communication that I was not sure I believed in and Tom was being asked to do things he had never been asked to do before. I just wasn't sure if he was really pointing to letters on the letter board or I was subconsciously leading his hands to letters. We practiced spelling his name, his address, typing colors – all content I thought he should know but really wasn't sure. We videotaped, not only to show his parents but so I could watch myself and see if I was doing anything that looked like I was controlling his hand movements. Despite our nervousness, there was a curiosity on my part and I really wanted to investigate this seemingly mysterious process. At times, I was convinced he was initiating the movement towards the letter board. I was also intrigued that he was actually sitting there allowing me to do this with him. From working with him in his employment, I knew if Tom hated an activity he would either get "stuck" or become aggressive.)

This went on for quite awhile with little improvement. I was never good at questions with a specific answer. Laurie hung in there, however, and we struggled together. I was dreading going into that computer room more all the time. She was too, I could tell.

I could not see the letters on the keyboard long enough to hit the right one. I could find it with my eyes, but it would be gone before I could attempt to reach it with my finger. By that time Laurie was asking me something else and I was still trying to find the first letter and it kept disappearing on me. You can imagine how frustrating it became, and I was not helping by becoming uncooperative. I really wanted to talk to her but didn't have any idea how to convey it. About this time chief facilitators (self-appointed ones) were taking pot shots at all of us in an unorganized fashion. It was most frustrating. At night, letters from the computer keyboard would flash in and out of my mind. They began to take shape in my head like a computer keyboard. In my mind's eye, I began putting together the letters to make words to say what I wanted to say. But the next day actuality came and I still couldn't hit the right letters on the keyboard.

Everything went too fast for me, and I couldn't keep up with the pace. Everything started falling apart for me then and I was again left alone with my chair and stupid buttons. The staff was concentrating on the more efficient ones. The newness was wearing off and now the "Doubting Thomases" became quite prevalent. Hearing staff line up on sides became a favorite pastime of mine. I wasn't so sure which side I was on either, maybe a little jealousy? Since sharing mental space isn't uncommon among some of the persons with autism, some of those vibrations were pretty heated, also some of us failures weren't very nice to the favored few. I feel bad about it now. FC went on among the winners, but the excitement wasn't nearly as high.

FC Was Investigated for Others

About this time my parents heard about this new fascinating mode of communication. Since my mother was Executive Director of Opportunity House, where I lived in one of the group homes, she felt obligated to explore it. Not for me as much as for some of the others who lived there. No one, not even my parents, thought I was a likely candidate. Everyone, for years, said I had the least amount of initiative of any person with autism they ever saw. I couldn't even scratch my nose when it itched or look in the direction of sounds that I heard. I wanted to but couldn't make my body answer my commands. People talked about this poor retarded soul like I couldn't hear either. They weren't trying to be mean, just thought there wasn't anybody home. They just didn't know how to ring my bell.

My parents and some of the staff made a trip to Maine to attend a workshop on FC. When they came back I didn't get the feeling they were very enthused. Especially my Mom, she has always been known to be a skeptical person and this was pretty far out there. I heard them discussing this topic and my Dad was obviously more inclined to be a believer. He is more of a far-out person naturally.

(Mom – I was not very impressed with what I saw and heard. Tom's severe apraxia, along with my knowledge of other persons with autism movement difficulties, caused me to reject the idea that

inside was a person just waiting to get out. I ask the same questions that people are still asking us. It was far out to me that using this method could tap this sort of response. I was so negative with my staff that Tom's Dad and I had a few words about it later.)

Another parent, Rena Gans, went with them to the Maine FC workshop. Her son Kenny was one of the better FC users at the adult work program. She was a believer and encouraged him even though he was sporadic in using it. She would tell of some pretty amazing things he seemed to know and my Mom was skeptically impressed. The big question was his literacy without the proper education. It hasn't changed much today. That is the first question everyone wants to know. I wish I could explain it in words that everyone could understand. It is being able to absorb information like a sponge and then bringing it out when you need it. The processing and formation is the problem. With me the information began to make sense when I began to actually FC. It has something to do with touch and relationship with the facilitator that started the rusty wheels turning. Some of us have developed a sense that most of you have lost long ago. To survive we can join with others in a mental space. Some of us do this all the time. I know this is where some of you will stop reading, but it must be said. Do not interpret this as not having thoughts of our own. We can pick and choose what information we receive and process. Combine this with what I said before and we can easily pull out facts that are remarkable to you. I will cover this more later in my book. Now back to my story.

(Sue – For Tom, learning to communicate with others and his environment came from a keen development of his ability to perceive electromagnetic fields. Due to the decrease in sensory interpretation in some areas, he has become sensitive to energetic frequencies that they learn to identify with and use as a form of communication. This is just like individuals who lose their sight will increase their ability to hear information not ordinarily heard by the average person. Learning to perceive subtle energy patterns requires a quieting of the linear mind which is constantly being bombarded with external stimuli and distractions. Through discipline and practice we can sense the quality of vibrations around us and begin to translate a

world beyond the normal senses we commonly live with. It takes us deep into the science of unity and our concepts of reality must shift. It forces us to release belief systems that favor separatist, divided, individualistic views that do not reveal a holistic approach. As we take this leap in our evolutionary journey, we will continue to experience and understand all that exists beyond the physical as having form, as having consciousness, as having life that creation is made up of a continuous spectrum of realities.)

My Mom watched the FC saga unfolding with interest, still skeptical. Thank heaven the adult work program pursued it with the favored few. You would be surprised at the amount of true FC taking place in spite of some pushing of hands. Most of we autistic knew the differences but it didn't do FC any good to have even <u>some</u> fakery going on. The people who sort of believed were really turned off. The sides grew farther apart and became whispers in the shadows. The big group in the middle were afraid to take sides and just ignored it.

Meanwhile, back at the campaign buttons table, I had mixed emotions about the whole thing. I knew it was real with some and I was jealous and scared they would point me out to try again. Failure was my middle name and I just didn't want to face it again. Good Old Thomas Scott Failure Page.

Most of the clients had feelings about the subject of FC. Some didn't want to hear about it. Some were scared to participate. Some made fun of the ones who were doing it. I was in the scared group; I really wanted someone to try again with me but was even afraid to admit it to myself.

Some of we persons with autism talk among ourselves via vibes and minds. We can sense one another's words without saying them. We talk in terms of vibrations that translate into energy forms. You do the same, only you don't recognize it. You have a means of speaking that we don't, therefore you haven't needed to develop this way of communicating. Kenny was the one I communicated the best with (some people with autism can sense one another's words). I confided this to him with much intrepidity. He felt sorry for me but agreed we were not in very good positions to fix the problem. It is not easy to communicate a desire when even your facial expressions are practically nonexistent. I remember how hurt my Mom was when she taught at my school and a staff member called me "Mr. Personality." She didn't mean it as a compliment and my Mom came home and cried. So I sat there and dreamed about what life might be, if I could talk, even if it was with my fingers.

Break Through, Message with Mary

What happened next, I wasn't there, but have heard the story told many times. Kenny was getting proficient, enough that he wanted FC in all parts of his life. It was important to Mary "the one they called the Queen," also. Somehow they managed to get a group of people together who worked with Kenny. A meeting was set up, partly to show off Kenny's skills and, hopefully, interest others in doing it. My Mom was invited. During the course of the meeting, Kenny asked my Mom specifically if she was FC-ing with me. As the story goes, she said, "Not really, Kenny." He then said," I think you should try again, because he is ready and wants to talk to you." My Mom was stunned and embarrassed. She said something like, "I will think about it." After the meeting was over, Mary came over to my Mom and asked if she wanted her to try. My Mom said go ahead. Kenny came back to the workplace and told me telepathically what had happened. I was horrified. Every day when I saw Mary, I was scared to death she might approach me. She carried around one of those laptop computers and seemingly chose victims randomly. In my head, I continued to put together the keyboard in case I ever got it together and had a chance to use it. In my fright I really kicked it into high gear and almost became manic about it. She kept passing me up, however and I relaxed. Maybe Kenny was not telling me the whole story.

One day, out of the blue, Mary was waiting for another person to come back. I was sitting in my usual spot. There she came approaching me with her scary equipment. I bit on the bullet and decided it was then or never. She was very nice and gentle. I was petrified! When she took my hand, the computer screen in my head lit up. Words and phrases came tumbling out. It was as if I were in a daze. It probably was one of the most emotional experiences I ever had. I don't remember much about it in detail. Now I am amazed I came as close as I did, in accuracy, with that little typewriter. I must really have been psyched.

Here is a computer copy of that event –

```
                    mevy)                              /- Tom
            (tom would you like to tell m1hello)/how are you/freedom
  .is holding your hand/this is like miracle/like healing for us/
  .'(tom what would you liketo tell your mom?)
  .  yes her tommy does know how to facilitate/just be patient/so

  like her to epetiomize  the question/reading minds likew some
  type of liar/just desehelp tom facilitate to his mom/seemom bite
  her lip cant stop the teazrs/let her cry for joy/seeall
  justticed just dues/kisss her gtears for me/mary hide pain like
  you are now/all great thoughts are startedx with teargves
  louylowry relly see great healing in your touch/you ar

  ves/lowry how do you like. my pupil mary/great subplot for movie/
  yes it really is me/do you like seeing me talk/inpedfdrr
  womtreery to facilitate lowry pleasequdytug    motcidu vm
  sf/just keep trying/it is going to take pupil lowry learning/aua
  way that is dear freinds/least favorite way to teach like mymom/
  she likes perfeitionb/answer lotro please yes fuovk hcpvi7
  repeojmn    sovovofno ' fofop
```

The rest of the segment will have to be what others told me.

Someone called my Mom and told her what had happened. She wanted to believe but was still very skeptical. Can you blame her? She had thought of me as severely retarded all my life. This was quite a jolt. They sent her a copy of my doings. She and my Dad were in awe but were still standing on the impression that it might be a hoax. I think they were afraid to believe. Most parents have been beaten down after suffering one bad experience after another. It is unfortunate because many good treatments are lost because of skepticism.

When I came back to the house that night I was scared. I didn't know how they might react to the news. My parents were excited but calm. They praised and made a fuss over the event. I heard them discussing how much a lap top cost and how they might experiment with the process themselves.

I Hit My First FC Home Run with Mom

Next weekend I went home and I could tell my Mom was gearing up for the big event all day. She was dreading it and I was sort of, too. What if I couldn't produce? I had not been very successful at my work program after my initial performance. I felt like a concert violinist with a cheap violin standing there waiting for the curtain to open. After dinner, the curtain opened; my Mom bit the bullet. She had even made out a list of questions for me to answer. Of course, they involved recall, my worst suite. (Nearly every facilitator falls into this pit.) They always want to ask a specific question of the past and are upset that we can't conjure up the answer very often. Our inability to deal with time makes this virtually impossible. Example – You may ask us what we had for dinner last night and we may tell you a food but we don't know if we had it last night or not. We are much better at conversations expressing feelings and telling stories as I am doing now. My Mom's strength and courage gave me the shot in the arm I needed. She kept them very simple with a word or short phrase answer. We really did quite well. Both of us were very excited and my Dad, the onlooker, was estatic. None of us had any idea of my potential, at the time.

(Mom – He may have felt strength and courage from me, but I felt both excitement and dread. I felt as scared of failing as he did. Every parent wants to feel they can do what others can do with their child. What if I couldn't measure up? What did that mean if I failed? I was warned not to test, but I had the need to prove to myself this was true. We used a crude, quickly put together, paper letter board. Good enough for a start. The session wasn't perfect, but I got enough to make me hungry for more.)

My output of thoughts was not very organized. They came and went with the tide. Sometimes I could ride a big wave and produce and other times it was a small ripple and petered out with little meaning. Everyone expected me to produce all the time. It was frustrating to us all. My Dad made a paper letter board for me since we had not bought the laptop yet. They didn't know the trouble I had seeing the small keyboard. I operated almost totally from the one in my head. It sure didn't help accuracy. It was like picking through weeds in a flower garden to read my talk. Since I didn't use the set keyboard much, only to get my bearings, I only looked at it occasionally. This was a big problem as it really fueled the flames of skepticism. I really appreciated my parents' patience and determination. They had tasted success and were psyched. It is really true we struggled to keep afloat. It was just like a colt when he is born and is wobbly on his feet. The three of us got better and better. I could do it with Mom pretty easily after a few weeks. It was heaven on earth for me. I could finally express myself to people, who really mattered in my life. We started expanding topics. They were surprised when I would verbalize something (my speech is very limited) and type something else. It soon became apparent the typing was the correct one. I guess it is like a stroke patient calling objects by the wrong name.

Many Staff Really Tried

Meanwhile back at the workplace, Laurie kept plodding along. I had "upped" myself in the staff's eyes (those who believed in FC as a viable means of communication). We had graduated to questions and answers by then. We were using the laptop and my accuracy was quite questionable. You really had to sort through the letters to find my responses. I struggled so, not really aware of my movement problems. Couple this with not being able to find letters with my eyes, and it is a wonder I ever got anywhere at all. There were several staff now who tried with me. I had varying success with them. I wish I could say everything they got from me was true facilitating. The truth of the matter was part yes and part no. Some people have such overpowering thoughts that it is hard to make ours known. The facilitator must open their thought channels. Some people push hands too. It is really frustrating to the user. Enough was true, however, to make me want to keep going. I looked forward to Laurie FC-ing with me. She was one who could keep the channels open, neutral and grounded. She wasn't the only one who could; I also want to give credit to all those who were honest.

It was starting to impact on my life. All kinds of things started going through my mind, especially at night as I don't always sleep well. This was all building up over a few weeks.

A Cry for Help Via FC

One day at the work place, between campaign buttons, Mary came to FC with us. In fact I don't remember much of what happened during the whole thing. People don't realize when a severe behavior occurs all our sensory channels shut down. All the things you say or do falls on our unseeing eyes and unhearing ears. I only remember remorse and panic. It is very difficult to think about it now. From what they say, I began running around chasing and hitting everything that moved. And I mean hard as I am a big guy. In fact I nearly hurt Mary. She was game though and when they had me in four point restraint, she got the letter board and with a freed hand I typed "get my Mom, I need to talk to her." They got her on the phone and she rushed over.

They obviously put me in an isolated room where I remained until she arrived. It seemed an eternity. I could not express all the feelings rushing through my mind. I was so ashamed and embarrassed for my actions. I wanted to cry but was unable to even do that at will. I felt like a whipped puppy waiting for the discipline to happen.

My Mom came in and gave me a hug. She looked pale and somber. I was both glad and upset to see her under those circumstances. There were so many things I wanted to tell my parents and I didn't know what was going to happen next. All of a sudden my Dad appeared on the scene also. My Mom had called him. I hadn't expected this and it really threw me. Most people with autism do not deal well with the unexpected. He asked if he could stay and I said no. I know I hurt his feelings and have felt bad about it ever since. He has always been supportive and I sent him away. I just didn't expect him to appear. Brave Mary came in with the laptop and she helped me to facilitate. Words again came tumbling out in a stream; I couldn't stop. My Mom sat there shaken and trying to be supportive. I was telling her my hopes and dreams at that point in time.

Here is a computer copy of that event –

```
TOM WHAT WOULD YOU LIKE TO SHARE?
MOMQUIETB YOUR WORRIES I NEED TO TALK TO YOU ABOUT GROWING UPHOW
CAN I TEASE LIKE THIS MOM I NEED BTO LIVCE ON BKMY OONOWN JUST
OLLIKE KILLING MARYS BACK TODAY I TRY TO TELL YOU THIS THE ONLY
PUPIL MARY CAN HELP ME TSALK TO YOU THE REALLY IMPORSTA NRT
WORDS I NEED TO CONVEY HUG BME M,ARY NOT PUPIL MARYS HUG THNTY
FRUSTRATES ME I NEWED TO LIFVV E ON MY OWN UJIJKUST LIKE REALLY
FRUSTRATED MEN DO ANSWER PLEASE MOM
TOMMY I NOT SURE HOW TO ANSWER BUT YOU HAVE MANY THINGS TO LEARN
BEFORE WE CaN DO THIS. CAN YOU HELP US?
YES DONT REASON IT THROUGFH I COAN EXPLAIN THE BREASON BUT FOR
NOW I NEED TO FREEVDOM ISA LIKE HUGGING MOM FOR THE FIRST
TIMEBTEREASEV ME WITH HUGS THAT DONT TTRY TO FREE MEB ANSWER MOM
PLEASE
IT WILL TAKE TIME WILL YOU BE PATIENT?
YOYES HUG ME MO M·
MOM I LOVE YOU YOU HUG ME IN EVETRY WAY HUGGI NG IS ONLY PART
OF YOUR ROLE OIN MY LIFE HUG ME .MARY FIXING IS NOT WHAT I NEED
MOM I HAVE TO MOVE OUT OF OHOUSE YOUR KINGDOM IS TRATO LARGE TO
HUG MY NEEDS HYES JUST FPOR TREATMEJNT OOR YOUR
FRUSTRAFRTRATIPOMN JUST UNDUE THHE KINGDOM AND SET US FREE
MOMVHUG ME MARY  TIGHTER THE BETTER
YOU THINK HUGS ARE POWERFULJUST GGET US OUT AND I WILL BE
FOREVER GRATEFUIL GET AJN APART.KMENT NEAR YOU HUG ME MARY
WOULD YOU WANT TO LIVE WITH SOMEONE?
JUST ONE OTHWSE R MOM YUESN YOYYOU CAN HEPOLP TEACH ME HOW TO
LIVE LOIULOOKJ HOW MUSJMUSDH INMLIKE LEARNING FROKM YOU GET
GOING MARY HUG ME FRGFFREEDOJJMMIS HUTGGINGVTHEB QUEEN OFR
TGFRACILITATIONB TRY HOT BATH MARY FOR YOUR BACK
LILIKEB THE WORLD HAS BEENHJ LIFTED FROM ME MOMI LOVEB YOU VERY
MUCH GOD HBLESWV YOU TRY TALKING TO HIM BEFORE HE READS THIS KW
KISS YOUR WORRIES AWAY MOM I KNOWBTRHIS WILL HAPPCEN NOW GO MARY
HUG ME
```

We were all basket cases by that time. Mom left, I had to stay there, and then Mary went home to soak her poor back where I had hit her. I feel so bad because her relationship with me was never the same. It is important I tell you how much she has meant to my life. She is a very sensitive person who all clients felt they could trust. She had the quality that gave you confidence because she believed in you. You don't know how many people think of our heads only as hat racks. She was able to bring out mutual trust, which I needed badly. The door she opened for me has changed my life and I'll always be indebted to her. She really tried but I could sense her fear after that. I could sense everybody's fear after that. They continued to FC with me but respected my moods and wishes big time. This was not to my advantage as I used it when ever I felt threatened. It was not something new as I had used it for years but this reinforced how powerful it could be.

FC Became a Way of Life at Home

Many times I wanted to do what most of the others at the workplace were doing. They seemed to have a much better life than me. Those whose movement difficulties were not as severe got to go places and do jobs where they could move around. Isn't it interesting if you can talk and move around well you are considered intelligent. Not only that, but they see that their life is better by all standards. How often I and others like me are left alone because we are not causing difficulties. After I began to show signs of life, the staff began to try to stimulate me at a safe distance, however, because of my previous behaviors. It was far to late by that time. I was much too set in my routine pattern.

I remember one time, they decided I could deliver papers. Probably I had agreed to it. I really wanted to prove to everyone, including myself, I could do it. Unfortunately I had to get on a van to go. I think I got as far as the door and then went tearing back to my chair in horror. My mind was willing but my flesh was weak. That was pretty much the end of the experiment. Let's not blame the staff too much; they didn't have the knowledge available we have today.

I don't think I progressed much at productivity. People did start seeing me as a person, however. I continued struggling with the laptop with varying results in accuracy.

Meanwhile, at home, Mom and I were getting somewhat conversational with FC. We had purchased a laptop by then. She finally came to grips with the feeling I was not her baby boy, but a real person who was not included in society. She always thought I was not being hurt by unkind things that were said to and about me. This was comforting to her. Now she had to deal with the fact that I was indeed hurt and very knowledgeable.

(Mom – It is true. The first time Tom came home for a weekend, after I had read the print-out from his work program, was indeed uncomfortable. I deeply, remember looking at him with eyes that were trying to comprehend a different person. What should I say to him? Did he want me to play the childish games, talk the silly talk, do the baby-like affection that was my way of playing with him a good deal of the time? Even though I probably understood and interacted with him better than anyone, this was a different kind of person. If what he typed was real, he must think I was very degrading in my actions. Was my need for being maternal manifesting itself in this unhealthy way? Here was a grown person from my body whom I hardly knew. It took some time for me to adjust and get comfortable with our new relationship.)

My parents had wised up to the fact that I needed a bigger keyboard. My Dad made one out of paper and mounted it on cardboard. They talked a lot about what was appropriate. Mom made dark letters and drew squares around them. It worked a lot better for me but there was no print-out. Therefore it became even more questionable if they were my words or hers. She wondered too, like all good facilitators. She religiously wrote down all my words and kept them just like a print-out. We both were pretty new at this.

Back to my poor Dad. He wanted to FC with me so bad. One of his characteristics is not doing things in front of others if he might fail. We used to sneak off to the kitchen when Mom was busy and try. Boy, were we failures. Mom would appear sometimes and offer a little tidbit of advice. That would end our short session pretty quick. If I got a few words, it would make our day. He stuck with it and after at least a year, we improved greatly. Many Dads never get to the place where we are now and I am grateful he hung in there. It finally became our way of life. I had a voice in the family.

(Dad – I was a failure at FC with a word showing up once in a while to tease me. I want to thank Tom for sticking with me. To FC you must establish a relationship of caring and a desire to communicate. The person with autism must have a lot of patience too. It was a long but worthwhile year and Tom's patience was phenomenal. WE MADE IT!)

A New Work Place for Me

Since I had very little concept of time, I don't know exactly when the following events took place. All of a sudden the adult work place was in turmoil; it was restructuring. People were all upset, some were talking about leaving and some were doing it. Laurie was one who did. I was really shook. Others did continue to FC with me. I really tried, afraid it would stop. It is really frustrating, waiting all day for someone to finally take some time to help you talk. Even that talk was not of my choosing. It mainly consisted of questions like "How are you Tom," "Did you have a good day," "What did you do today," "What did you have for lunch?" Routine questions with routine answers and recall! recall! recall! They are all testing questions and bring pressure. We can't function well under pressure. I would try to make a stab at it and once in a while hit Bingo. It must be frustrating for the facilitators. Many of them give up. To me it means they don't care enough about me to pursue the issue. That can't do much to enhance a relationship. It is not the only factor with people not being able to FC. The issue is very complex and individual.

Meanwhile, at about the same time, I heard people, including my parents, talking about starting a work program at Opportunity House, where I live. It was to be for the "losers", meaning the ones who weren't going anywhere in their work programs. I figured that included me, the big loser of them all. I had mixed emotions about it. Of course "Mr. Personality" couldn't express them even facially. On one hand, it could be a new beginning but on the other, it could really confirm my low self-esteem. It didn't happen for awhile, anyway.

My parents and I were pretty conversational by then. They kept me informed of the progress of the project. They had mixed feelings about this new venture, also. They were talking retirement. They had kept going for years for me, as they weren't satisfied with what was happening in my life. This threw another road-block in the path leading to their golden years. It must have taken a lot of effort and planning. They would run things by me and seemed genuinely interested in my responses. It was my first taste of feeling like a person of worth. The taste was strange but good.

Again, I was scared. Part of me wanted to remain safely in my old chair, but the FC experience had struck a chord of something I had not felt before. People, at least some people, had made me feel alive. I liked the feeling.

In all the hubbub of talk, Laurie's name kept coming up. My folks were impressed with her work and caring at the work place. She was not there anymore. Things fell in place eventually and Opportunity House's workplace, Page One, opened its doors to six losers. I had been brought along with the plans and had visited the site many times.

It was and still is an unconventional place. We each had our recliner/rocker, if that made us happy. If anyone didn't like that kind of chair, they got one to their own individual liking. Therefore, we had our own built-in comfort zone where we could go in our free time or if we were having problems – a built-in safety zone where we could go if our senses were askew. I liked this idea but I was scared it would turn into another place I couldn't get out of. It was one of the first times I decided I was going to beat this devil called autism. It took a lot out of me. Sometimes I won and a few times I lost. The winning ones kept me in the ball game. It got easier as time passed.

(Mom – The "new" workplace came about because one of Opportunity House residents (not Tom) was losing his placement at the other adult program. He was losing it because of severe challenging behaviors. Opportunity House, at that time, had several more residents who obviously were not doing well at the other program.

We, Opportunity House, decided to try a new approach in dealing with their individual difficulties. Our intent was to set up a calming, non-threatening environment to start with. (About every other method had been tried). We decided to try and include each clients sensory needs as much as possible and work with them instead of trying to make them come to our way of living life. That is when some good things started to happen with most of them. I must say the former program was very supportive and cooperative. They still have the best interests of these individuals at heart).

Enter Laurie, Glad to Have Her Back

My parents had gotten interested in the sensory approach as well by this time, and they wanted to incorporate it into our work place. Mom had contacted Laurie, who had gone into business for herself. I was really glad to see her again. She was to train the staff at Opportunity House workplace to FC with those who were using it. It was a struggle again. More conferences and workshops for my parents and staff. Laurie inserviced Page One workplace staff and tried to set an example for them. Actually some of them came through. The whole atmosphere of the place was new and exciting, too exciting some times. We all came with our old idiosyncrasies and behaviors. It still was frightening and scary, at times, when a client was having a bad time. Most people don't spend a good portion of their lives worrying when or if they are going to get hit, kicked or bit. I'm talking other clients not staff. The poor staff were kind of funny to watch. They were running around like chickens with their heads cut off. Sometimes, many times, confusion reigned. Soon it calmed down and some semblance of order took place. It wasn't perfect but a darn sight better than anything I had before. I was getting out and doing things with staff that amazed even me.

I had joined a FC group at my former workplace. It is a group of FC users who meet to talk with one another. Each has their own facilitator, and it is a place to express oneself. It is led by a non-autistic person to stimulate conversation. Sarah, a teacher there, would meet us and take me in and facilitate with me. I was thrilled at first to be involved with other FC users in actual conversation. After a few sessions, she informed my parents she could no longer facilitate with me because I didn't go to that agency anymore. I could go but had to provide my own facilitator. This was the story of my life, two steps forward and one step back. I panicked again but my Mom asked Laurie to go with me and she agreed. You people may not know that we are all quite aware that nearly all our relationship friends are paid to do everything with us. How would you feel if that was the way you would be living all your life? I have accepted this. It will not ruin my life but it is humbling. I do know that some of my paid friends have real feelings for me.

I began having feelings about some subjects and topics they were discussing at the FC group. It was the first time I felt like asserting my own feelings against those in an authoritative position. It made me angry when the leader would try to make us do things like verbally talk or move when I knew it was impossible for me to do it. I made him highly uncomfortable by getting up and walking out or becoming behaviorally scary. Laurie wasn't too comfortable either. We both questioned how much the leader really knew about autism. I quit once and then later decided to go back. When I did come back, I could tell he was less than pleased to see me. He took care of the situation all right by pushing me over the edge and insulting me. I was so upset! To this day, it was one of the most traumatic and humiliating experiences I ever had. I was not blameless, but I certainly lacked the social experiences to handle a situation like this. I never went back to that group or associated with him again. What I got out of it was a reputation of being a "prickly pear." It was another learning experience for me!

Darlene Brings Sensory

Our workplace was coming along OK for us and my parents felt we needed some heavy-duty sensory work. Laurie said she had worked with an occupational therapist at another agency and they worked well together. I guess the contact was made. Thus enter Darlene! I'll never forget meeting her for the first time. She is not a shrinking violet and the place reverberated from her aura. She was friendly but used good judgement. I don't know how to describe her but her presence certainly makes an impression. Her energy filled the room and I felt we connected immediately. I never met anyone who stirred up my energy like that before. She and my beloved Laurie came to our workplace a few times a week. You will never know how much we looked forward to those days. She consulted with the powers that be after a few sessions and told them in sensory terms what she thought some of my problems were in those areas, the results being a daily massage in a darkened room with some weird music playing. It felt good but was strange and again I was not always cooperative. At that time, Darlene had been exposed to FC but had not facilitated, I think. It did not take her long to become proficient. She is easy to share mental space and energy with. Since my vestibular system is bad my folks learned a lot, which improved my life greatly, an example – they never knew I had always been carsick and now they always let me ride in front. What a relief!

(Darlene – The vestibular system located in our inner ear is our guidance system through gravity and space. It gives us information about where our bodies are in space and whether or not the environment around is moving or still. It can be thought of as a foundation or orientation of the body in relation to surrounding space. The vestibular system receptors, which are located in the inner ear, also tell us about the speed and direction of our movements. The vestibular system influences many areas including eye movements, posture and movement, balance and equilibrium reactions and coordination of the two sides of the body in gross and fine motor skills. It is also closely connected to the auditory system, better known as hearing and listening. The vestibular system shares the same cranial nerve with the auditory system. The vestibular system is sometimes referred to as the "ear of the body" because it detects motion. In an initial OT assessment of Tom, I noticed a disordered vestibular system was a "roadblock" to function. This "out of balance system" in conjunction with poor feed forward from his body in space receptors known as proprioceptors in his muscle, tendons and joints lead to significant problems for Tom. In my practice I have often observed disordered vestibular systems as part of a sensory profile for people with the label of autism.)

Laurie and Darlene Made Quite a Team

Laurie and Darlene made quite a team. Laurie was the stable branch of the tree and Darlene was the wind and other elements rustling through the leaves, shaking things up and making it interesting. Pretty soon there was trouble brewing. We clients became very jealous of the attention that they gave to everyone except ourselves. Those with initiative started chasing them around with letter boards. Those, like myself, with no initiative just sat and sulked. We talked to each other through vibes and it got a little heated at times. I was accused of getting more than my share of attention because my parents ran the place. They were probably right but I was not going to complain. Things finally settled down to a routine.

My abilities started getting better. I was able to maintain my focus for longer periods of time. Events began to chain for me and some semblance of togetherness started to take shape in a limited way. Part of the problem was and still is, in a smaller way, that nothing stays constant. One minute everything is on go and the next everything is falling apart. Compounding the situation, you never know when this is going to happen. It really confuses people who work with you. It also affects the validity issue. A person can get a valid answer one minute and then sometimes the fog sets in. For awhile the reliability becomes an issue. This causes a lot of anxiety and behaviors to occur that are not understood by people who are around. There are many days when the whole day is like a fog over London. We, also many times, have a real delay in our responses and emotional output. It can build and build . Then just a slight trigger can bring forth an enormous outburst. That is when people will say, "What is the matter with him?" They don't have a clue that what happened was hours ago. Remember we have trouble understanding the time concept.

Sensory Also Was Becoming a Way of Life

Back to Darlene and my massages. I got used to them pretty quick. They felt so good and I could feel the calming affect they had on my system. This feeling didn't last very long sometimes. It seemed to depend somewhat on the level of anxiety I came with. Most people with autism are at a high anxiety level all of their lives. During a massage I could feel my space enlarge and peaceful thoughts come into my head. I even got so my hands and fingers would relax. She was the only one that could provide that service so it only happened about once a week. I was really jealous of that special time. It really bugged me when a couple of other clients would keep interrupting my personal time.

Darlene taught Laurie how to do the sensory stuff and Laurie taught Darlene how to FC. We had the best of both worlds. Darlene taught my Mom the massage technique and I began to get it most every day. We were on the right road at last, but it didn't solve all my problems immediately.

I Have Better Thinking but Not Control

My thinking became better organized, but my control was still bad. Things that used to **not** phase me started to bother me no end. Things like other clients taking my food at lunch. My initiative problem kept me from swatting them at the right time like I should. It would build and build until much later. Then it would all spill over and I would start chasing and hitting. It would become "what's-the-matter-with-him" time. I wanted to cry out, "What's the matter with **you**? You let him take my food and expect me to do nothing." We would all lose in the end, except the jerk who got my food. I now know that he had many problems of his own, but at this time this is how I felt.

This happened one time when Laurie and Darlene were at the workplace. They thought they had the magic touch, but got a quick lesson in what the phrase "beyond the point of no return" means. In the middle of the episode, they decided to give me a calming massage. Well, I was certainly in no condition to receive the benefits. They no more than got started and I became violent. They tried to stay calm, but it was sheer terror. I felt exuberated from their vibes. Another bad scene for me. When it was over, I was very humiliated. I could have alienated the best friends I ever had. I hated myself more than you could believe. Would they come back? If they did, would they ever work with me again? The episode with Mary came to my worried mind over and over. Why couldn't I control my behavior? It really sent me into devastation. Of course no one knew this. They thought I got real pleasure in seeing everyone scramble. (Occasionally, I did, if I felt they deserved it.) Not this time; I was really worried. To my relief they were back on the job as usual. Wounded a little, perhaps, but game. It took a while for them to get their confidence back, but over time we regained our relationship. The true test was over for then.

(Laurie – When Tom would have an aggressive episode, we would assume that his arousal level was so high that he was in flight-fight-freeze – a state of panic and lack of control. It was his body's attempt to protect from a perceived danger. In Tom's case this panic would be fight – and fight he did. What we learned over time was that he calmed more quickly when he was left alone. We tried to cut off any stimulation that, if he tried to process it, it would send that arousal level up to panic level again. His system was just too overloaded. Auditory, tactile, even visual input was either cut off or kept to a minimum. What are typically calming strategies were not effective for Tom. Only when he calmed, and his arousal level came down and allowed him to process and organize input, would we talk to him and try to find out what exactly precipitated that event.)

(Sue – I had read that the autistic experience emotions in a limited way and I began to understand why that interpretation may seem valid for some who are in this state of being. Although Tom was clearly experiencing emotion, his ability to discern, and integrate the information of the experience was greatly hindered. He would resonate with a particular emotion but didn't always have meaning attached and couldn't find a place to put it. It was chaotic at best, creating continuous uninvited explosions of violence and rage at his entrapment. In addition, it was impossible for his body to reflect what was going on inside, leaving him with a vacant affect that further alienated him. These were followed by deep remorseful feelings that those who were willing to care at all would continue to be afraid and would most likely write him off, leaving him further in despair with little hope of making connection between the worlds.)

The work program kept changing staff and supervisors. The FC component kept falling apart. Then someone would come through again. FC is very much based on relationship and trust. This doesn't happen overnight. Considering the difficulties people with autism have developing and keeping relationships, this is a lot to ask of them. This happens a lot more often than it does with you so consider how painful it must be. Another thing that happens to us many times, staff as they leave, promise to come back to see us, call us, write us and it rarely happens. We wait and wait for the contact and finally give up hope. I know they mean well when they promise, but it doesn't do much for our self esteem.

(Mom – One of the real challenges of group home living is providing caring, stable, long-lasting staff. Most of us are uncomfortable when faced with establishing new relationships. We know how difficult this is for this particular group of challenged individuals. They have many problems in building trust with people who work with them, yet we haven't found a way to keep many good staff long term. It is frustrating for everybody concerned).

New Skills but New Worries

I began to realize this new-found skill of FC was great for most purposes, but it had its downside, too. I had never before worried about some of these things and now I could put things together better and really worry about them. I am a born worrywart just like my mother. Worry became one of my worst enemies and to some degree still is. I can pick out the smallest detail and grow it into giant proportions. We have a lot of time on our hands to do this. My parents soon realized this and encouraged me to talk, ad nauseum, about things that upset me. Encouraged might not be the right word – **strongly encouraged** might be better, **made me** sometimes would be even more correct. I wasn't always happy about this. I beat the tar out of a lot of letter boards. In fact, many went sailing across the room. I finally realized that it was in my best interest to get things out in the open. Many times I had misinterpreted information that had upset me and it was good to get things straight. My parents learned when I was really upset was not the time to straighten things out. They now can tell when to move in and when not to. Now I don't throw the letter boards as much but just get up and leave the room when I'm not ready to talk. By the time this book gets out, I have no idea what my methods will be. They seem to change as I meet new horizons.

All General Staff Don't Take Advantage of FC

The work program went up and down with the change of staff. The staff in charge come with their own aspects of what is important in a vocational program and charge ahead with their own ideas. Interestingly they have a gold mine here in us and never think to tap into our resources. Two of the clients can talk on a limited basis and others can sign on a limited basis. Then there are three of us who can FC and they are not taking advantage of it. When they do, they are more concerned with the validity of our talk and not what we have to say. Some just find it interesting. Some people just want us to say something funny like we are entertainers. Then they rush to each other and repeat and laugh like we are freaks in a side show. Sometimes we do want to be funny but let us pick our times to joke around, like you do. It is real hurtful to hear people making a joke out of something you thought was appropriate and serious. I know we haven't had a lot of worldly experiences, but we need help in gaining that experience, not a jolt to our egos. Please don't think I am talking about everyone. There are some who try hard to communicate with us and use it properly.

I Recognize My Behavior

My behavior was improving, at least in my mind. It wasn't perfect by any means, but the reason behind it was more recognizable. I didn't hold it in as much and then explode. I would just explode on the spot but not nearly as often and not in a violent way. Staff were still leery of me. That upset me more now. I really began to see what negative impact it was having on my life. I began to understand how to be reasoned with and tried to cooperate. It all depended on who tried to reason with me. I had to have a relationship with them and feel they cared about me. It certainly didn't work all the time, but I started having feelings that I might conquer this horrible thing that was holding me back so much.

I Got Interested in Others' Lives

Another change that began to happen in these last few years was my curiosity in other peoples' lives. I started to wonder what some of my friends and staff were doing when they weren't with me. I have the ability to tune in on their lives by concentration and did so sometimes. That is not very nice I am told , but it is too tempting not to do so on occasions. Then, I would tell them something it should have been impossible for me to know and they would be shocked. I know many of you will think I am delusional and that is your prerogative.

(Laurie – A big milestone in Tom's growth in communication and language skills was his beginning to take interest in others' lives. In his beginning use of facilitation, Tom's language was very egocentric. Unless something happened to him or by him he didn't appear to comprehend events. The first glimmer at Tom's beginning ability to perceive and understand events that were happening to other people was his asking "wh" questions. The first time he asked, "What did you do this weekend?" it was a celebration in language growth. One time, I was one host in a progressive dinner party on a Saturday evening and was a bit nervous because one of the guests was a smoker and I had just moved into a new (and smoke-free) home. Not only was Tom interested in the affair and asked many questions about it but also asked if my friend smoked in my new home – something I had not mentioned to him previously. While this ability of Tom's to know facts about life that I had not told him was a bit disconcerting, it was also an indication of how close our

relationship had become. I do think it was one tool that Tom used to learn to look at events with taking another's perspective and eventually develop a broader view of his world.)

I Wanted My Eyes Fixed First

My parents had been following the auditory training thing with interest. They always thought I had trouble with my hearing all my life. I, like most persons with autism, displayed inconsistencies in being able to respond to sounds. That made my ability to act on them delayed. I'm not sure yet if it was my hearing alone or if my movement and visual senses were involved also. I strongly suspect the latter. The thing that held my parents back was the outside chance that my behaviors could get temporarily worse. They had enough of that old chestnut. My behaviors were finally getting better. I'm stressing my negative behaviors a little too strongly, I'm afraid. They certainly did not occur daily – just often enough to keep everyone on their toes.

One night at home, my Mom asked me if I wanted to try the auditory training. I responded, "Fix my eyes first." Even I don't know where that came from as I don't remember dwelling on my eye problems that much. When you have never seen properly, how do you know you have any more difficulty than anyone else? I do remember watching other people do things and wondering how they did that. On the other hand, people watched me doing my specialty feats, such as walking on the top bar of the swing set when Mom wasn't looking or bouncing exactly 20 ping pong balls all at once, and wondered how I did those, also. It became harder after adolescence to do any of my former specialty feats. Everything slowed down and that is when I became "the big blob."

Back to my eyes. My parents asked Laurie and Darlene if they thought it was worth pursuing. I think it was Darlene who said she had worked with a client who had gone to Dr. (William) Padula. She said she would ask about him. Later she told my Mom he was controversial but thought we should let him evaluate my eyes. I was kept up on the goings on and hoped they would follow through.

They didn't always, as I said they picked their treatments cautiously at this stage of my life. They did make the appointment, however.

Now time for me to worry. What would he do? What would he think of my method of communication? Could I control my behavior? Would he hurt me? Would he ask me to do something that I couldn't do? He doesn't know me so how could he understand any of my problems? People who had been around me for years didn't understand anything about me. I wanted my eyes looked at but suddenly I was scared.

Those Wonderful Words, "What Do You Think, Tom?"

By this time I was getting quite conversational with Laurie and Darlene. My validity was being checked out daily. I could hear them discussing my stories and remarks and keeping a careful record of them. I know it is necessary but how would you like to have everything you said recorded and scrutinized for truth and validity. It is a little humiliating especially when you have trouble with recall and are not always correct. Sometimes, some of us with autism make up things and hope we are right or at least get you off our back. Rather like you people, don't you agree? But of course, we aren't supposed to be like you in that respect. We should only be like you when you say so. It does irritate us and occasionally we play games with you and refuse to cooperate.

(Laurie – In the early days of Tom's facilitation, we were always searching for proof of authorship. We would ask Tom questions and analyze his responses: did he type something we didn't know before, were there any commonalties in his spelling and style of writing across facilitators? He was so effective in subjective and emotional language, why did he have difficulty with telling me what he did on previous evening or even what he had for lunch? It was extremely frustrating, especially since every once in a while he would, out of the blue, relay information unknown to us. It took us a while to finally figure out that Tom has a poor concept of time. Events don't appear

to be temporally organized for Tom. It was so difficult for Tom to pinpoint a specific event in time, that I'm sure he would just make something up. It was a milestone for him to learn to type "I don't know" and an even bigger milestone when he would type "I am not good at answering questions like that.")

As I was saying, I was becoming very conversational and the four of us, including my Mom and sometimes my Dad, would try to engage in some meaningful conversation whenever we could. This is what helped me the most. I was being included in ordinary, life conversation with real, so-called, normal people. The words "WHAT DO YOU THINK ABOUT THAT, TOM?" became the most important words of my life. The canned speeches about making choices and "how was your day?" are OK and necessary, but the interesting part of FC is sharing our lives with each other. Even today, not many people, except the favored few, do this on a regular basis. I crave and fear this will be taken away. I have committed myself to losing autism as much as possible and now have a lot of difficulty retreating back into my autistic comfort zone. It leaves me in the middle with no place to go when things get really bad. You have no idea how much control I have to internalize to keep from doing things that will get me in trouble. I feel like a bottle of soda that has been shaken but the cap is still on.

Discriminating Between Self and Non-Self

I was still having a lot of trouble discriminating between self and non-self. This means a person doesn't know who or where he is in relationships with others. I will expand this subject later. Many thoughts are invading our mental space and ours are trying to get known. This causes a lot of confusion for both the user and the facilitator. This is where a lot of facilitators give up. They think they are talking to themselves and sometimes they are. We just can't get our message through. This is really bad when a user does not have a clear picture of self. This can develop but it takes work on everybody's part. The better the relationship the two people have, the better chance it will happen. There must be trust and the positive expectation of eventual success. Without this you will possibly be cheating or fail. We think very highly of the people who stick by us and believe in us. They are our heroes.

Syracuse Conference

One of the most important things I did to boost my morale was to attend my first FC conference in Syracuse. I feel it is important for everyone, if it is possible, to visit another part of the country and see what they are doing. In my case it was the FC conference, which was designed to include the FC users in several parts of the program. Since it was such a controversial subject, I wanted to see for myself what they were doing elsewhere.

It was a thrilling experience. It turned out to go beyond my expectations. The first session was a meeting of FC users who **wanted** to meet one another. After we assembled in a large room, we were asked what topics we would like to discuss. We then broke up into smaller discussion groups of our own choice. There seemed to be a lot of chaos as we did this, but it all worked out great. I ended up in a group of about eight to ten users. It was tense for me at the start but the vibrations they all put off were so positive I soon relaxed.

They all introduced themselves and the rest was talking about our topic. We all exchanged names and addresses and one father put them on one sheet. He then ran out and made copies for all of us. It was the beginning of a long list of long distance acquaintances. During the discussions, everyone was given a chance to express their opinions. It was the first time I had a chance to talk with a group of strangers from around the country who had autism. They were polite and friendly and also eager to meet new people who had autism. The whole conference was geared to the needs of these people. We met with others in hallways, hotel lobbies and several places. It was good to see and hear others in person instead of reading about them in an article. I had been around a quite a few people with autism in my life but this was my first chance to get out with my new-found ability to communicate with them. I recommend it to all, but read about any conference first to see if there will be activities that will draw other persons with autism. The annual FC conference does that. I feel it gave me a real boost. I came back feeling there was hope and not just a few of us here at home. I now know it is used in many other countries and is growing all over. Of course the conference was geared to the parents and professionals too. I attended some of those sessions. It was a good feeling to discuss them afterward with my parents.

Early Spiritual Feelings

I also started to feel my spiritual being beginning to expand. I always had a deep belief of a higher power and was in awe of the universe. When I was quite small and used to come to my Mom's nursery school class which was held in the church, I would wander away from her room. Something would direct me to the sanctuary, which was a complicated and faraway place to get to. My spiritual guides showed me the way. I would lay in one of the front pews and would become very peaceful inside – I loved it there. I'm not sure of its purpose, but I loved being alone with my thoughts, disconnected as they were. My Mom would discover me missing and after a while come and retrieve her property. I had to pass by the church secretary and minister's office to get there. They considered me weird and chose not to get involved. Since I never bothered anything, they probably thought I could use all the religion I could get.

Dr. Padula and High Expectations

The big day came for our appointment with Dr. Padula. I say "our" because all of us involved were very nervous about the ordeal. The entourage consisted of Mom for moral support, Dad for strong arm support and poor Laurie who was to FC with me. We moved as a group to support each other. Dad and I sat in the car until it was time to go in. I'm sure I was noisy as I get that way when faced with new unpredictable situations. That doesn't help my supporters' confidence. I don't always know when I am making those kinds of sounds. They just come out. I was ushered into a small room with scary looking equipment. This isn't good for someone like me who wants options to escape if he has to. Mom did her usual morale-lifting support, smiling and rubbing my back and telling me how great I was doing. All well meaning but grossly overdone. Dad was doing his usual low-key profile, but ready to move if necessary. Laurie was trying to be perfectly composed but kept licking her lips. They were probably dry from fear. Her reputation was really on the line if he didn't believe in FC. It seemed forever before he appeared.

He was rather a small person compared to us giants. He had very intense dark eyes that I was fascinated by and drawn to. They seemed to look into my soul. I knew at once my life was going to change forever. I knew he knew more about me in a few minutes than most people who had known me all my life. It wasn't long before he recognized I needed space and changed us to a much bigger room. He talked directly to me and pretty well ignored the others. This was unusual in itself. I wasn't used to this. I felt totally responsible for my responses. It really frightened me but I liked it. He was asking me to identify things and numbers. I don't know whose eyes I was using, mine and also anybody's I could hook into. I have the ability to do this. He was fascinated by my ability to answer correctly without apparently looking at the object. I didn't know everybody couldn't do this. I always thought I was doing what other people did. I didn't realize people might think I was cheating. I think I became aware of this when people started to examine me with more scrutiny. They were puzzled by this and became more aware I was different. People ask me now when I started to do this. I don't know. I didn't think in those terms until later. Also Laurie didn't know I had this ability and was avoiding looking at anything. She didn't want him to think it was her, by any means. He tried to trick me once by holding up a blank page. I could read the number he had written on the back of the page and FC-ed it to him. He was pretty impressed and perplexed. He knew something unusual was going on. He also had me walk a couple of miles – at least it seemed that far. He was just watching me and watching me. Some of the time he put strange glasses on me. They really made the world look odd. I wasn't sure if I liked it that way. This was all making me highly uncomfortable. It doesn't take much to do that. I had no idea where we were heading. I had had it by then. I took a chair over by Mom. Unfortunately, it was close to the wall. I couldn't take it anymore and started hitting my head on the wall. Thank goodness it was almost over anyway. My Dad took over and he and I went to the car. That really upset me. I thought that was the last time I would see Dr. Padula. He was cool as a cucumber on the outside, anyway. He must have had some experience with customers, but probably I was the biggest. I knew he thought I needed glasses. I heard the word prism but wasn't sure what that had to do with anything. Mom and Laurie were in there forever. When they came out Mom said, "I needed to pick out some frames for glasses." She picked out several and brought them to the car with a mirror. I guess he wasn't through with me yet. I was relieved. I tried them on in the car. I helped pick out the ones I liked even though I couldn't see them very well with my own eyes. We headed back, all four of us. I remember Laurie asking for a mint, she said her mouth tasted terrible. I think we all consumed them; it was nerve racking but we were all impressed with Dr. Padula and his methods. A tired group went home.

That was the start of many visits to Guilford. The glasses didn't come for awhile. The strange looking ones came first. They were really weird looking, like something from outer space. They changed how everything looked. The floor looked no longer tipped and the walls were straight. It was scary to see things that way. I wasn't sure if I liked it or not. They made me walk different and my body kept fighting to resume the old position that I was comfortable with. They didn't make me wear them very long at a time. No one insisted I wear them at all, but I heard my parents talk about how expensive they were. They were not complaining but I felt an obligation to try, especially after my performance at the office. My lack of initiative kept me from refusing too much anyway. It got better the more I wore them. If we were out in public, I sure was noticed. Between the glasses and the noises, when we were out, people probably thought I was truly an alien.

The other pair came soon after. They were more comfortable to wear. They too straightened out the world. At times it was almost too much to handle. It was exciting though and I tried my best. It didn't take long for me to wear them all the time. The world looked bigger and scary with them on. Things shattered like glass when I tried to focus on anything too long. It happened before the glasses but was more obvious now. The glasses helped me see better, because they helped me focus. It made the breakup more apparent. (Dr. Padula explains the breakup on page 13. There it is referred to as spatial organization). Now I would get a glimpse of something whole every once in awhile. That was a strange experience for me as nothing ever stayed constant before. I had always seen bits and pieces of things like faces, but not the complete object. When objects move, like people, it was even worse. This was overwhelming now. After a couple of visits Dr. Padula put some dark stripes on the nose side of the glasses. They seemed to help the convergence of my eyes. The world narrowed down to a manageable size, and I adjusted much better. This didn't happen over-night. It is not like you just put on glasses and bingo, everything is perfect. It is sometimes a tedious and sometimes even painful experience. Like Dr Padula says, the eyes are just cameras, but the big stuff takes place in the brain. I not only had a malfunctioning camera, but the developer in the back was hardly producing pictures that were in focus enough to be recognizable.

(Dr. Padula – The use of prism glasses began to have the affect of not only organizing what Tom was seeing, but it was soon apparent to the professionals who were working with him, as well as his parents, that Tom had a better ability to control his own emotions for periods of time during or after using the prism glasses. This may seem a rather unusual statement to make; however, we must place ourselves in this imaginary environment of what it must be like to have a severe state of visual fragmentation from post trauma vision syndrome. I propose that it is like being in an environment with hundreds or perhaps thousands of flashing lights and with the speakers all around turned up to full volume. For Tom, the visual world constantly broke up into pieces and parts. As he would move his head or eyes, these pieces would shift and swim about in an uncontrollable manner.

Excessive stimulation can very easily agitate the visual system, as well as the entire neurological system for a person. Having to deal with this for minutes, hours, days, or years at a time can easily cause emotional problems and anxiety. By calming the visual process, it is not unlikely that the anxiety can be reduced and in turn produce a more controlled emotional state due to organized sensory processing.)

My whole thinking processes continued to become better organized. I think it was the result of all the therapy treatments I was receiving. I was already aware that my orientation was different than ordinary people. I never really felt that I was a part of this world. My thinking was different. I had no trouble identifying with spiritual matters. It was so simple and became so clear, like talking to guides from God's kingdom. They instructed me and encouraged me in how to deal with my present dilemmas. They would help me make decisions for my future. One of these discussions was to get rid of the autism barrier as much as possible. That was one of the most important decisions of my life. I had no idea how much work that was going to be. In fact, I might have backed away if I had it to do over. My life has not been the same since. It was so scary – I had no idea where to start. All the guides did was provide the idea, drive and determination. They do that, you know – you have to work out the details. I started really concentrating on my more mystical side. The whole realm of spirituality opened up to me. My internal eyes could see it all. Words sometimes would come pouring forth through my finger (FC) without my realizing it. Can you imagine what my poor parents thought? I wasn't sure how they would receive the information. Again my Dad was more open than my Mom. She is a good "kid" but things like this throw her. She let me have my head and didn't try to shut me up with her skepticism. It took her a while to adjust to this unusual thing she had given birth to. It was about this time I started writing serious poetry. I had dabbled in some pertaining to autism but now things pertaining to spirituality and higher powers flooded my conscious and unconscious mind. My parents were amazed and silently coming to understand me better. They questioned me about my beliefs and compared them to their own. Believe me, they didn't always match. They listened to me intently and privately said I made good sense. Of course I did, I was getting mine from the true higher powers. There are so many mistakes in most religions. (Well that should eliminate some more readers but stick with me please.)

Dr. Padula Suggests a Friend

This was about my third visit to Dr. Padula's office, it still was not a comfortable trip to make. Both my parents looked forward to it and dreaded it at the same time. When I am nervous, everyone is nervous. I don't think Laurie always came at that time. When my Mom was ready to leave, Dr. Padula asked my Mom if I ever talked about mystical and spiritual things. My Mom was shocked and said, "Yes, all the time." He said he was treating another autistic boy who FC-ed. His mother reported that he did this a lot. He asked my Mom if she thought I might be interested in meeting a friend of his. This friend, he said, worked in the field of energy balancing and healing. My Mom didn't have a clue as to what he was talking about. By this time she was getting used to my far-out ideas and was willing to accept anything. She said she would talk to me about it and let him know. I didn't exactly understand what it entailed, but I did know about energy. I said I wanted to explore the friend and her theories. It took a while but finally a meeting was arranged at Dr. Padula's office after his hours. This in itself was different for me as I cling to my routines and this was definitely not in my time frame. I need a whole lot of preparation to internalize a change. Even then I need to be having a good day to make it. I must have been destined to meet this challenge as I transitioned OK.

I Meet Sue and Another Door Opens

It was already dark when we got there and that was different in itself. The office looked very different, Dr. Padula looked very different, every thing looked different. This may sound like a foolish thing to you, but to me it was a traumatic change. If it had not been for all the arrangements made to get me there, I would have ran to the car big time. I had started to converting to flight, sometimes now instead of fight. I just hung onto my security blanket (a piece of bubble pop packaging paper) and kept telling myself my parents wouldn't let anything bad happen to me. My Mom always arranged the chairs now so I wouldn't be very close to the wall. Smart move on her part.

When I sat down and got my bearings, I saw Dr. Padula and at the end of the room I saw a pretty lady. She didn't look unusual but her aura filled the entire end of the room where she was sitting. The aura was very beautiful, all whitish and gold. There were many rays coming from it very ethereally. They were almost vibrating. It was both calming and frightening at the same time, but very intriguing. Dr. Padula in his usual calm and quiet manner introduced Sue to us. At once I sensed calmness and my guides assured me all was well. She appeared to be calm but probably wasn't on the inside. We connected immediately but hadn't a clue what to expect. She, I'm sure, hadn't met anyone like me and I sure hadn't met anyone like her. I had always been able to see auras but nothing like the one on her. Dr. Padula has a good-size aura but nothing like hers. They asked me some questions but I'm not sure what they were. I was too preoccupied with the entire experience to do much concentrating. My answers were probably pretty nothing. She asked my parents if they thought I might lie down on the massage table she brought. My Mom said we might try but laying on strange tables wasn't my best suit. They hauled out a folded-up something from the far wall. I remember they had trouble getting it undone, which didn't give me a bunch of confidence that it would hold me. With some coaxing and moral support from my Mom I did finally get up there, heart pounding. There was conversation about pillows under my head and knees. Also, if they thought I might like a blanket over me. After watching TV, I was beginning to think I was going into surgery. Everyone took their protective places. They did it in the most discreet manner but everyone knew what was going on. Sue turned the already low lights even lower. She also turned on some music similar to what Darlene plays when she gives me a massage. Her aura grew even brighter when the lights were down. It sort of enveloped me. I was receiving strange feelings all over. Not unpleasant, just strange. It was a bigger-than-life feeling. I felt like I was light and floating. She started at my feet and manipulated them with her fingers. So far so good! She was very confident and reassuring. She kept telling me to just lie there and she hardly touched me at all. Occasionally she would do things with her hands. I could see spirals of light from her fingers. Her aura changed colors several times from blue to shades of gold. I was extremely comfortable with this. It was like I had been waiting for it. My spiritual side took over. It was over too soon and I wanted more. I don't think it was over too soon for my parents. They could see none of what I had described. Their concentration was on my behavior. What she was doing wasn't in their vocabulary. At the end of the session, she asked me if I wanted to see her again. I really did. I knew I had encountered a soul mate. Everyone seemed pleased. They made arrangements to meet again.

Staff Changes Slow Progress

Meanwhile back at the work place, more staff changes had occurred. It really kept Darlene and Laurie busy trying to train new people. I don't think you understand how difficult it is for us to adjust to new staff. It is tough for you to make a move from place to place and have to make new friends. When you have a deficit in social abilities like we do and then are expected to accept all new people in our life, there is a problem with the picture here.

Controversy Stops Progress for Many

Also, It is not like everyone falls right into the concept of sensory integration and FC. A large percentage of the people reject it right away or it takes some long time doing. I hope some of the pundits and adversaries of FC and sensory integration realize how many lives might have been saved or made better but by their rejection. Why do they care so adamantly, anyway? Could it be they are afraid of their professional stance? Why are they so inflexible? It sounds like an autistic trait to me. Even if it only saved a few from desperation, isn't that enough to give it consideration? Sometimes I wish their motives were scrutinized as much as they scrutinize us. Not many, if any, could stand up to the microscope we are subjected to.

Some of the staff changes were beneficial to us, but most were not. Most of the staff are naturally skeptical and don't want to seem like kooks to their peers. Even though they were all told of expectations of the job, many say what they think is necessary to get the job then worry about it later. Poor Laurie and Darlene have to face everyone alike. They expect us to be trainers or guinea pigs. I try to cooperate but sometimes the vibes are so bad that I know we are never going to get anywhere. Once in awhile a natural comes along. Sometimes I think they are embarrassed too because they must face the others that can't do it. You have to be a strong person, who doesn't succumb to others' possible contempt. It is sort of a no-win situation for us. Never forget: A relationship with us is a very vital part of it all.

The same thing goes for sensory training. Some people go through the motions of massage, brush and press, etc. while talking to their friends. We must concentrate for it to do us any good. It is hard when their minds are on other things. Keep in mind we may not look like we are concentrating, but we are. Our confusion between self and non-self causes us much difficulty to not follow the other person's thoughts. Many times I have told Laurie, after her giving me a massage, that she was thinking of something else. I have been pretty specific about her thoughts. It blew her mind at first, but she grew used to it. It was especially convincing when I typed Laurie's thoughts to Darlene. I think "feet-on-the-ground" Laurie is still confused about this.

I especially want to mention my true friend, Delicia. She is House Manager at the home where I live. She is, what I said above, a true natural. She is willing to share of herself like friends do. She is the kind of person who a lot of people depend on. I know a lot of staff were critical of her efforts. They were also the ones who, when they needed to know what I wanted or what was the matter, ran to her to come and try to find out. She has always been intuitive and tried to think how I might be thinking. I want to give her due credit. If it weren't for her, my life at the group home would still probably be the pits. Every FC user should have a Delicia where they live. I want to give some others credit, also. Some have really been good and left. I do wish I knew what happened to them. I guess I wasn't as important to them as I thought. Some want to FC but come with so much baggage of their own or deficits of their own that we can't make the connection. Sad, isn't it? Anyway Laurie and Darlene have a tough job. I can feel their enthusiasm go up and down.

I Show Interest in Books

I have also discovered books and talking books. I had been able to read head-lines in the newspaper as long as I could remember. No one knew it of course. How could poor retarded me do such a sophisticated thing? Even at the school I attended no one thought I was capable of doing anything academic. Because of my severe sensory problems, "Mr. Personality" probably didn't show the right normal signs. If I never have to match blocks again, I could care less. I hope I never have to hear the words "Good Job or Good Boy" again. Good Grief, I'm not blaming anyone. They only knew what they knew. People like me are resigned to mediocre tasks like setting the table and taking out the trash. If they are truly like me and have severe movement problems plus – they can't even do that.

I'm not sure how I got started reading books. I think it was when I FC-ed my interest in the development of the old west. My Dad shares the same interest. He started reading a book recommended by a friend. It was called *The Frontiersmen,* by Eckert. It was about Simon Kenton, a friend of Daniel Boone, and Tecumseh, the famous Indian Chief. It had a lot of situations to talk about. We would stop every few paragraphs and discuss what was happening. It was new to have someone want to hear what I thought about books. We read several about different subjects. Understanding what was said was easy but knowing the characters' feelings was fun. One time, I suggested we read a book by Rudyard Kipling. We went to the stacks

in the library and picked out his famous book, *The Light That Failed.*
It was about a newspaper illustrator in the days before news
photography who did drawings of news events and especially war
coverage. He was quite famous, but begin to lose his sight. He felt
sorry for himself and deliberately lost his life. When we finished the
book, I typed the following paragraph:

He could have been somebody in the world even if he were blind,
but he didn't try. I am going to be somebody in this world even though
I'm autistic. I am going to beat it. I am doing what I can to prepare
myself to meet the challenges before me. It is my very special handicap
that will allow me to succeed where others might fail. This is my
destiny. To take advantage of it to help others with handicaps and
others without them. It will be soon, but slow progress it will be.
(*Dad – I wanted Tom to include this story in the book because it
really confirmed to me the commitment he had been showing.*)

The Interest May Come from Past Lives

It was about the same time I began having flashbacks from
previous lives. They really consumed me for a good portion of the
time. They were very vivid. I really didn't want to talk to my parents
about it. They had never inferred they believed in that sort of thing.
As I have said before, I get real ornery when I have something on my
mind and don't express it. After a lot of prodding, I told them that
and a lot of other things that I can't go into here. They were stunned
and, as usual, my Dad came around first. I don't understand what the
big deal is anyway, a large percentage of the earth's population believe
in reincarnation. There is no question in my mind. Many of my interests
and characteristics stem from past lives' experiences. Besides affecting
my book choices, my poetry and prose started to take on a different
motif. It became more spiritual and deep with meaning. Many times,
I now feel it was channeled. I seemed able to move in and out of the
two worlds, this world of yours and the spiritual world, which I was
more comfortable in. This was not with ease, however; I really didn't
like your world much. It was filled with all the things that assaulted

my inner being. It frightened me to the extent of constant retreat. When I realized what was happening, I panicked more than once. This is not a good thing when you are blessed with my size. I would worry myself into a frenzy thinking about all the responsibilities that came with my chosen goal – to be able to function in your world. There were times I just pushed the spiritual guides aside and thought, "I don't think so." They were supportive and gave me my space for a small while, that is. Then they would come back with a vengeance. My supporters knew nothing of the battle going on with in me. They were mostly concerned with my conflicting moods. I was not at all out of the woods behaviorally and there were memories of the past that will always linger. I have to live with that.

Professionals Encourage Me to Express My Beliefs

I was blessed with a group of professionals who gave me support even though some of them certainly weren't in tune with some of my thinking. Talks with Darlene, Laurie, my Mom and sometimes Dad about my spiritual side and beliefs became the most important part of my existence. I would think about it most of the time and then have to wait until someone came and took time to talk to me. It couldn't be just anybody either. Not that just anybody could talk to me anyway. It would build up in me like the tide. Sometimes when we would settle down for a talk, I would be higher than a kite. Overpeaked, you might say. I would go running from the room to my safety zone chair, leaving behind a group of perplexed supporters. It would produce overload affecting my brain and ruin my entire day. "He is edgy today" is what they would say. It was usually from dwelling on something and not being able to get it out in a timely manner.

Darlene seemed to understand my thinking on those matters. She helped fill in some of the gaps to the others. She didn't seem to think I was off the wall at all. Much of what I was saying ,via FC, matched many of her studied beliefs. She said she had some other clients with autism, who talked via FC, as far out as me. They seemed to express many of the same beliefs as me. She gave Mom some books on the subjects I was interested in. They were interesting and mostly reaffirmed my beliefs. Not everything in the books are correct, however. We had many interesting discussions on these issues and I amazed them with my insight and knowledge. Why not, mine came directly from the source. I'll never forget Darlene inviting me to a party at her house. My Dad took me, not sure of what we were in for. Her friends all accepted me and all my idiosyncrasies. They tell me I was the hit of the party. That was a first for me. Usually I was body guarded. I want her to know how much I appreciated that. It really boosted my self-esteem.

The Work Is Hard if You Do It Right

Darlene started working with me on some sensory equipment like big therapy balls. She was concerned with my vestibular system. This type of work really frightened me. Just sitting on a therapy ball and bouncing would be like you being tossed high on a blanket. You never know where you are in space. She tried putting me in all kinds of situations and positions and extending my arms and legs every which way. I had no idea where any part of my body was or where it was going, especially if she wasn't modeling it. I was too preoccupied with what I was trying to do to hear many verbal instructions. I would often try to see any outstretched hands or any other clue to see what she wanted me to do. I was quite prepared to cheat any way I could. She and Laurie worked as a team and it was work. Often the three of us were sweating before it was over. The best thing was the way they let me critique the session, stopping every so often to ask me questions about what I was experiencing. That was very important to me to feel a part of the process. Sometimes the sessions were pretty short and sometimes lengthly. It all depended on my tolerance level. The world was now starting to move *with* Tom, not making Tom move with the world.

(Darlene – Intervention, targeting the troubles Tom was having pulling together his postural control, related to moving and seeing in a dynamic environment (everyday life) was key. His disordered vestibular-proprioceptive-ocular triad was our starting point for treatment. In our early sessions, the therapy ball was the piece of equipment that allowed for the type of input Tom seemed to need. The opportunity to provide graded input to the vestibular system, a variety of planes of movement and at a variety of speeds was essential and possible on a very large therapy ball since Tom is a very large man. Tom's vestibular system was overly sensitive to movement input and, therefore, I had to move cautiously, following his lead, always trying to set up the "just right" challenge but careful not to push him beyond his limits. This was hard work for all involved yet we were all willing to take the risk. Tom's nervous system's low tolerance for movement input, as well as his difficulty initiating movement, changing direction and speed and maintaining his body in a position other than seated with feet on the floor made for a great challenge.)

Involved Completely with Sue

We were now involved with Sue on a regular basis. Still we were meeting in Dr. Padula's office after his regular hours. We were having sessions with all of us. The sessions would start out with them probing my brain with questions mostly about spiritual matters and how I perceived the world or should I say worlds. I mean your physical world and my nonphysical world. My nonphysical world was the one I lived in most of the time. I could tell Sue was really intrigued with me. She and I were intrigued with one another. We seemed to talk the same language. How good it felt to talk to someone with ease. She was still working on her certification in energy work. After the first session she asked my parents if she could work with me alone. They said OK, but I could tell they were in a shaky mood about it. I could feel them in the hall ready to intercede if necessary. I was starting to gain confidence, but they had no way of knowing. It was a very spiritual experience being with Sue alone. She could summon and synchronize our energies. I had no trouble keeping up with her. This was a world I was quite familiar with. The energies were not completely organized but I understood them. I had used this concept all my life in various forms. How I looked forward to these sessions. After a couple of times Dr. Padula didn't come to them anymore. Sue asked my parents if we might be interested in her using me as a subject for her dissertation paper. She needed this to complete her certification. They asked me since I was to be the center piece. I had no qualms about it since I knew she was sensitive and truly cared about me.

At all these sessions, we talked (I with FC) and shared beliefs about spiritual things and religions. I do mean shared as I felt a part of all conversations. I was a big contributor and my ideas were always taken seriously. They learned from me and I from them. It was a great release for me. Sometimes I came with a lot of baggage and it didn't always turn out as perfect as it sounds. I might be noisy and banging on the FC board. She was very cool about it and I know she could feel vibes that others couldn't. Sometimes she would take my hand and meditate. She would tell me to center myself. She would suggest that, in my mind, I plant my feet firmly in the ground. I instinctively understood what she meant by grounding but not the image. Sometimes when she was doing her work, she would ask me to make mental images in my mind but I can't conjure up any on suggestions. I don't know how to do that even now.

One night she said she would like for us to come to her home office and in the daytime like regular people. That again assaulted my autistic trait of sameness. I was really shaken up. At that time, when I was shaken so were my parents. You can't imagine how much preparation, how much accommodation goes on to accommodate the slightest change. We verbally rehearsed ourselves to death. Made sure we had my favorite mints and packing paper (popping paper), promises of a donut after the session was over. It is worse than packing a diaper bag for a baby. Then we were on our way with me terribly noisy and they terribly apprehensive.

We arrived and her house was very beautiful. It was very calming in design and color. It was big and spacious, which is good for me because I get nervous when I can't see a way out. We set up shop at her big marble dinning room table. I calmed down and the session went well. Her therapy room was up three flights of a curving stairway. All the times we met there, I never did figure out which floor was which and which way to turn after I got to the bottom.

I grew to love that house. Much of my spiritual development took place there. She helped me to analyze and coordinate my thinking. I could talk to her freely about my conversations with the spiritual guides and what I knew about the spiritual world. She would ask questions about my beliefs and in the true psychological form make me think out my own thoughts. She also suggested books that she thought would fit my way of thinking. They were always my beliefs, not hers. The beliefs were there before she came along. She only helped me organize them.

Professionals Who Work Together

Meanwhile, I was wearing my glasses all the time now. Also I was wearing the funny ones nearly every day while my Dad took me on long walks. I can't say I ever enjoyed the corrective ones. It could be I knew people were staring, but I think they did me some good. My eyes would go in and out of seeing differently. They would change on me so often that it was very confusing. Occassionally I would think I saw things correctly, but it was fleeting. It was a guess anyway since I never knew what correct was. Dr. Padula was now working with Darlene, who was coming with me to FC. My parents felt that vision therapy should be done at Page One and not with just them doing it all the time. Darlene and Dr. Padula were interested in combining the vision with occupational therapy. How nice to see professionals working together. They started to do some visual things which combined movement and I can't tell you how difficult they were for me to do. My mind told me how simple they should be, but again my body rebelled. It really struck home how handicapped I was. I really tried hard to cooperate. They praised me for the most insignificant details. I accepted it, for I felt I deserved it. I was really clueless as to where any part of my body was in space. Couple that with my vision problems and you have a real mess. Some things they tried had an impact and some probably didn't. I'll never forget the bumble ball. Darlene found it somewhere. She has bags of stuff that most people wouldn't see any use for. This thing shook, played music and giggled. They would place it in my hands and require me to get in different positions without dropping the darn thing. It was a good thing it was a short session as it made a nervous wreck out of me. Very often it took two to complete a therapy task. Laurie was game and learned all the routines from Darlene. On the other hand, Darlene learned all the fine points of FC usage from Laurie. They made a formidable team.

(Darlene – As an OT it is my role to screen vision and note possible issues. As previously mentioned OT had identified issues with Tom's vestibular system, which has direct influence over ocular motor control. The vestibular sense responds to body movement through space and change in head position. It automatically coordinates the movement of one's eyes, head and body. These were all areas Tom was having difficulty with. Therefore, it made sense to make the referral to Dr. Bill Padula, a local neuro-develomental vision optometrist, for further evaluation and treatment of his visual system. Fortunately, I had the opportunity to accompany Tom to his appointments, which allowed for an area for direct consultation and team intervention. Together, Tom, his parents, Bill and I planned and probed strategies, problem-solved issues and celebrated the changes in posture and control that resulted in more quality performance, for example, the ability to demonstrate arm swing while walking or independently pulling up his pants. However small these seemed to Tom, we saw these changes a as progression in a positive direction. Most remarkable was that Tom's impressions of what was "wrong" with his vision-movement system was exactly what our clinical findings did confirm.

Proprioception is the term that refers to sensation received from specific receptors in the muscles joint and tendons of the body. It tells the brain how much muscles and joints are moving. Therefore, proprioception tells you how and where you are moving without needing to look. Kinesthesia is the sense that combines proprioception and touch (tactile) sensations to tell the brain about movement of the body parts in relation to each other. The body needs sensory input from these senses to make constant "subcortical" (unconscious) readjustments to be able to know where you are and move efficiently. These senses are the basis of body image. Since Tom has generalized low muscle tone, his brain works hard to get a mental map where his body is in space and how it is moving. Since often he has trouble initiating movements, when he can get moving the feedback from these body receptors is less than adequate. It is as though the feed - forward and feedback system is faulty from the cable company and the picture is fuzzy. From the person viewing Tom, his "body clueless- ness" may appear as though he doesn't want to move, he can't move, or perhaps when he does move, it lacks rhythm timing, therefore, appearing to lack coordination.)

Keeping Up with Breakthroughs

It was about this time I began to have breakthroughs. I probably always had them but they went unidentified, even by me. I think it was work with Sue when I began to realize there was a pattern here. By breakthrough, I mean, everything seemed to be smoothing out emotionally and otherwise, then I would start having small uncontrolled anxious periods. They would be triggered by practically nothing. They would accelerate and become more frequent until people would become most irritated with me and sometimes I would have minor behavior problems. People would be nice on the outside but I could tell they were anything but pleased on the in. You really can't fool many of us, but thanks for trying. I tell by the eyes mostly, but the way you move and touch me plays a big part in the total picture. My senses may not be intact, but I am very aware of this aspect of life. The vibes tell it all. Back to the breakthrough, it would be like a crescendo in music, peak and then when it was over, I would take another step in progress. They would last in length from days to weeks.

When I first had these spurts of progress, Sue was not with us. If she had been, life would have been much simpler. She was able to talk with me and all things seemed to fall in place. The thoughts she had were calming and made me feel like I had control. My mother was pretty good at this too, but Sue added another dimension. She gave me energy therapy that brought me inside my body and it gave me a feeling I had never had before. I will tell you more later, but this was the beginning of how she held it all together. Remember I said she was the glue.

(Sue – As Tom began to express his ideas about his spiritual experiences, it gave me the opportunity to affirm his knowledge of multi-sensory, multi-dimensional reality. Bridging his realities helps him feel safer about being more connected to his physical existence. Through validation, affirmation and energy work, his emotional body began to interact more effectively with the next layer of denser energy of the physical body. This created a "softer" more flexible flow of information and energy within the circuits of his energy fields. This helped to remove the harder, more brittle reactions coming from his emotional feeling centers. He began to exhibit more control over his outburst of anger and became more cognitively involved with understanding interpersonal relations. At this point he certainly began to have a "smoother" ride!)

My Breathing Problem Discovered

Now is the time to introduce Mike Nelson. He was brought in through the backdoor. That is not an insult. It means we needed his specialty, physical therapy, to solve a life-long problem. Dr. Padula was allowing Christine Nelson (no relation to Mike) to use part of his office space when she came. This was every other year, since she moved her practice to Mexico. She is a well-known and respected occupational therapist, who was seeing people in the area. He asked my parents if it was all right if she saw me. He had told her about me and she was interested. It was another of those times when patient and therapist hit it off right away. At the meeting, the entourage included Laurie, Darlene and my folks. Dr. Padula stepped in once in a while. She asked me, as well as the others, questions that gave her an idea of how I function. She was a master at preparing me for anything she did. She always explained what she was going to do and asked if I could cooperate. I did and even I was surprised at what I let her do. I laid on the massage table and let her manipulate my upper body into positions that it had never been in before. She seemed to be interested in my breathing. They all discussed my normal shallow breathing and my inability to breath on command. Also, they talked about my oxygen flow to the brain and blood in my body. I had never been able to blow either, like candles on my birthday cake. It doesn't mean I didn't breath, but I had no control of it. She gave Darlene a few pointers on exercises and suggested we get someone involved who had training in respiratory therapy, I think. How could a simple thing as breathing have such a profound effect on someone? I could tell she was intrigued by me and asked for some of my poetry to take back with her. I may not be much, but I do leave an impression. You can take that any way you wish.

Mike Becomes Part of the Team

On the way out of the office, Darlene ran into a man waiting with another client to see Christine. She stopped to talk with him. Little did I know how important he was to become to me. That was Mike Nelson a physical therapist.

When we got together the next time, we critiqued the visit with Christine. Everyone was excited with the new-found information and how it might apply to me. I think both Darlene and Laurie felt they were learning a lot through these experiences with me. This is very important to me because my mission in this world is to give knowledge of autism back to the mortals who don't understand. One of the pieces missing was the breathing problem. Darlene mentioned the man in the office. She said she knew him and thought he could fill this piece of the puzzle. My parents said contact him. She did and "voila" – here comes Mike.

(Mike – I first saw Tom at Dr. Padula's office in December of 1996. It was a quick glance. He had been the previous appointment with Dr. Christine Nelson to an appointment I had with another client. He walked through the waiting room with his father about 10 minutes prior to his mother and my colleague and friend, Darlene Talavera OTYR/L. It was a pleasant surprise when I saw Darlene walk into the waiting room with Mrs. Page. She introduced me to Mrs. Page and told me they had just talked about me in the consult with Dr. Nelson. Everything happens for a reason. This was my first introduction to Tom and his parents. Darlene and Jo Page said that they would be calling me to see if I could be a consultant to Tom's program. I was to be the NDT component that the team was looking for to complete the areas of intervention for Tom. NDT is Neurodevelopment Treatment Approach, developed by Berta and Karl Bobath in London, England. Christine Nelson is a NDT coordinator instructor from Mexico that comes back to Connecticut to provide consultations to some of Dr. Padula's clients. Dr. Nelson's eclectic approach to treatment utilizes some of Dr. Padula's Neruo-Optometrics and many of the principles of NDT and Neuro-Optometrics seem to combine well.)

I wish just one of these professionals entered my life easily. It is embarrassing to say how bad I behaved. Everyone told me the proper things and prepared me accordingly. Still the old feeling of failure loomed up as big as ever. One flashback after another occupied my being. By the time he got there, I had convinced myself this session was going to be a failure. To make matters worse, everyone hovered around wanting to see how this would play out. He looked harmless enough. He did all the right things, shaking my hand, looking confidently in my eyes, treating me like a person. When I say shaking my hand, I mean he did all the shaking. I rarely know where my hand is, let alone being able to put pressure where it should be. I had no idea what he might ask me to do, but past experiences had taught me that I probably couldn't do it. I hated showing everyone in the world, one by one, how I couldn't do anything. He was nice looking and the vibes told me he was gentle but strong. I just hoped he could hold me up if necessary, and I knew it would be necessary.

After about three tries, I finally made it into the sensory room. By tries, I mean, not being able to leave my chair. When I got there, I'm sure my noises were very distracting. I kept one foot out from under the table just in case I had to leave. He played it real cool, I don't know what he really thought. He accepted FC like "doesn't everybody." He and Darlene made me feel as comfortable as they could under the circumstances, but I was already higher than a kite.

We got a few sentences out and I was out of there and back in my chair. By this time my Mom came in and convinced me to return. They finally got me to do a few things on the big red therapy ball. He put me through a few physical things to see how I moved or rather how I didn't move. Then we sat at the table and discussed what had happened. He always told me (in adult terms) what he was going to do next. I appreciate people not talking babyish or not getting their faces in mine or raising the volume of their voices like I can't hear. He was surprised at my ability to give good feedback. I must mention that I made several trips back to my safe chair in the other room, intermittently. Good thing Mom was around to coax me back. The session was short but I could tell he was intrigued. It was breath mint time again as we were all exhausted. My Mom handed out more mints than I care to think about.

(Mike – Time passed and I finally got the call to come, and met Tom and his family with Darlene. I was not sure what my involvement was going to be but from past experience with Darlene as a friend and professional colleague I knew she has something in mind. Tom had already been exposed to a therapy ball program in his sensory programming with Darlene. My first role was to expand the familiar ball work to more complex programming that would improve his posture and motor responses. I believe that I was chosen to be a member of this team since I had previous experience with FC energy work (including manual therapies of MFR, CST) and sensory integration and have worked with persons with autism ranging in age from childhood through adulthood. Darlene knew my background and also knows my personality. If she could "rope me in" I would be committed to Tom's progress and programming for as long as needed.

Upon my first visit, Darlene and I co-evaluated my involvement. She showed me what was presently being done in the areas of massage (manual work), sensory and communication. I could tell from the beginning that Tom and I were going to hit it off. Here was a man, a year younger than me, that was totally intriguing and bright. He FC-ed with Darlene and Laurie full conversations with me regarding his feelings, and I never felt I was communicating with anyone less capable of decision-making than myself. It totally blew me away when I realized that Tom had only been communicating in this way for a few years. I was told that Tom had some violent tendencies and in my own typical manner shrugged my shoulders and said so what. We all have our differences. I had been around children with severe behaviors for years, so this was not even a remote concern for me. I already know enough to get out of the way and enter personal spaces with respect when appropriate. It is the same level of common sense that applies to all people, not just our friends, that have a label or identified "problem." Personally, I find that the aggressive and challenging behaviors of a person with autism or a related disorder are easier to interpret than a child with SED (Severely Emotionally Disturbed). I am convinced that there is a reason for all of the behaviors that a person with autism presents. They may not be rational in our minds, but I believe that they hold some level of rationality in the mind of the person displaying them, even if it is a reaction or an over/under arousal response to something in the environment that we cannot see, hear or interpret.

I guess I ramble on here because if the general philosophies of all the individuals involved are similar then we stand a chance of success. One more comment on behaviors. Tom used to hit his FC board a lot during facilitated conversations. The force and vocal sound effects associated with these motions were intense and could be interpreted as major signs of aggression, but I did not react and it just didn't seem to matter. After a few sessions, Tom was apologizing to me for the loud banging and sounds. I remember telling him that it did not matter to me. He continued to explain that they were energy bursts that he could not control but not to be afraid, he was not going to hurt me. I found it amusing since I never felt he would even think of hurting or aggressing toward me. I do not know if that was just being stupid or just believing in Tom. For the record, I have been hit, scratched, kicked, bitten etc. etc. many times in my career. Some were predictable, some were not. I just always felt safe with Tom.

Growth Is Frustrating

I was getting even more sophisticated in my thinking and expanding my world. People who knew me and could talk with me via FC were including me in their conversational world all the time now. The professionals and my parents were picking my brain on more profound matters. They were quite interested in my unusual way of thinking and especially my views of the spiritual realm. They were not necessarily their ways of thinking and wondered where it was coming from. I'm not exactly sure myself. Sometimes the words just come into my head and out my fingers. I am aware of my surroundings but deep into my spiritual side. I love those kind of discussions. They are very satisfying. At the same time I was having a lot of turmoil. I seemed to be growing rapidly intellectually, maybe that isn't the right word). Maybe it should be developing the intellect that was already there. My lack of worldly experience caused me a lot of trouble. My emotional, social and other systems were not keeping up. I was ying-yanging it all over the place. I could become very angry for almost any little thing. My inconsistency, for sure, was pretty unbearable for the people who loved me the most. An example: I threw a fit on my Mom's birthday because Dad forgot to get a proper cake. He tried to remedy the situation by substituting something I thought was ridiculous. I threw a class-A tantrum and besides scaring everybody to death, everybody ended up blaming and mad at each other. I felt bad and stupid about it the next day. I spent a whale of a lot of my life at that time, feeling sorry and apologizing.

(Sue – As Tom became more accustomed to experiencing his emotions (energy in motion) it was like opening rooms in a mansion

that had never really seen the light of day. Brilliant possibilities were before him. Choices, ideas, relationships all began to flood his conscious awareness. Quite a lot to deal with, but he truly learned to "trust the process"!)

Fear of Losing My Special Gifts

I realized I had come into this earth place with some very special gifts. Peoples' lack of understanding me and my special gifts caused me to develop them to a higher degree. Even though it caused me not to fit in, I really valued them. I was torn whether to proceed in my mission to rid myself of autism. I was afraid I might lose my special gifts in the process. They were very instrumental in holding myself together, even in the inefficient way it was. What if I lost them and didn't make it into your world? That was so scary, I didn't even want to think about it. I told some of my professionals and they said they didn't think that would happen. What did they know? One day, when I was out at Sue's, I was all worked up about it. My Dad had to take me out and walk around the house a few times before I could even talk about it. She told me to consult my spiritual guides and gave me a piece of paper with the words "Trust the Process." It helped me and I still have it on my bulletin board. To go ahead was one of my toughest decision.

Fear

I fight you so often,
I feel I know you very well.
You are not a welcome visitor
in my being,
but you are usually
present in my soul.

You stigmatize me
and halt my progress.

77

You keep me from completing
my missions here on earth.

Constantly, I must guard
against you.
You cause me to do the things
that are hurtful.

I will be bigger and
stronger than you.
I will not allow you to
run my life any longer.

Oh, how I wish I could
carry out this thought.
My mind flows on
knowing we will do
battle again and again.

Strengthen me God to conquer
this flaw in my character.
Let me do away with this
guest in my house.

Meditation Helps My Behavior

I also started seeing the negative side of my behavior. It was holding me back in every way. I made a commitment to myself to overcome my physical aggression. First I had to identify what caused it. I needed spiritual help. Again the guides never tell you much that is concrete. They sort of do the psychiatrist bit. They put questions in your head to make you do the work to figure it out. It is the long way around but I guess you profit that way. Personally I would like a break and a short cut now and then. I really got into meditation and ask for some quiet time each morning. We got some appropriate music and my Mom even voiced over the tape "Ocean Waves" with comments like "relax Tom" and "listen to your inner self." I know this sounds weird to some of you but it really helped me. I asked for (Sue's suggestion) a square of soft cloth in my favorite color, aqua. I fingered it while I sought guidance. This whole scenario was strange to most of the staff, but they went along with it anyway. After all, my parents were the boss, and they were sick of my behaviors. We didn't go into a lot of explanation. When you work with people with autism, nothing seems too strange after awhile.

I got better at getting into meditating the more I practiced. The music and cloth helped set the mood and cut out the distractions. It gave me a set time to summon up my spiritual help and I looked forward to it. A lot of plans were made at those times, some I could carry out and others gave me a lot of trouble and still do. After a while I didn't need the cloth and now I don't need the music. I just need some quiet time and I kick right into it, most always.

Attacking Problems During Physical Therapy

Meanwhile, back at the ranch, Darlene and Mike were putting me through the paces. Darlene and Laurie were massaging away and putting me through all kinds of things. We didn't have a massage table yet and many things were done on a mat on the floor. They were somewhat limited as I still couldn't force myself to lie on my stomach. I feel just too vulnerable and have the feeling I couldn't get up if I had to. It is just like a nonswimmer trying to float on his stomach in the water and can't do it, panic sets in. Breathing is already a problem and it seemed to make it worse in that position. They would ask me to do a lot of things that were to make me aware of my body parts and space. It took an incredible amount of concentration for me to try to comply. Sometimes I could do it after a long delay while my mind thought and planned it all out. They gave me a lot of positive feedback for these tiny steps. Other times they just tugged and pulled me through it and that was no easy task. It is a good thing my professionals all have a terrific sense of humor. That is really an important part of therapy for me. I give good feedback most of the time. It is important to tell them how it is.

Some of the sessions my Mom or Dad would attend. It is not always good to have too many people there for me. I find it too distracting and am always wondering what they think. It is worse when they come in the middle of a session. It really interferes with my train of thought. Lord knows I have enough trouble just getting a train of thought. Sometimes though, I want them to see the new me. I just want to be asked. It is so hard for my Mom not to help me when I am having trouble. She is unaware of the cues she gives unconsciously. Usually I suck them up too, as by that time I am getting desperate. It is hard on both of us. On the other hand I really want her there, as she is my real soul mate in this world.

(Mom – This is frustrating for all concerned. Some days Tom wants me there. I enjoy it and feel it is a learning experience for me. Other days he is not as well "put together" and just my being there puts extra pressure on him. True, I'm sure my "Motherly clues" are quite apparent to all but me. Again, we have learned to follow Tom's lead.

It must sound as though we are giving in to his every whim. It would have to me 10 years ago. Hopefully, we are making these accommodations now to help him learn to make more adjustments in the future. We are not sweating the small stuff. There are enough times he has no choice but to accommodate life now as it is. At this time, we are seeing many glimmers of it working).

Integrating Vision with Movement

Dr. Padula was starting to work with Darlene on integrating my vision with movement. They had my nose on the wall with my finger tracing a piece of tape on each side, or something like that, or had me lying on the floor twisting my body parts in different directions while looking at a small flash light or bright colored objects. There are many other such exercises. I kept Dad and Darlene busy making all the contraptions needed. It became obvious I had severe depth perception problems, also. I couldn't even find the ball on the end of the stick that Dr. Padula was always holding up for me to focus on. The only way for me to find it was with my finger then my eyes would follow and get a glimpse and I do mean short glimpse. I believe I have walked miles for him to observe. It is really difficult for me to look at anything except my feet and where they are going when I am moving. Therefore my head is always down. When we take walks it is not unusual for my folks to keep saying, "Get your head up, Tom." It comes up for a few steps, but I have to concentrate on it so hard that I can only maintain it for a short time. Part of it could be habit and I really don't know which is which. Dr. Padula says my midline, the one down through the top of my head, is not where it should be. For explanation of Midline Shift Syndrome refer back to page 13).

My Professionals Go with the Flow

Mike was coming on a regular basis now. I could usually stay intact for a whole session. Not so many trips back and forth to my chair. One of the secrets of my progress with all my professionals was their willingness to go with my flow. At my size, they didn't have much choice, but they all learned when and how to coax me gently back when I couldn't take it. Sensory overload is not at all uncommon with many of us. We really can't help it. Not that we don't ever use it for an excuse, but I know, in my case, it is usually real. I need my space and time to recover. I am getting better at this all the time.

Sensory Room Gets Changed

Sometimes in the realm of things we made a change in the room where most of the sensory stuff took place at Page One. All of this sounds so trivial even to me that it is hard to understand how it could possibly throw me. But throw me it did. The first time I was shown the new room I rejected it completely. I ran down the hall and stood where the equipment should be. The staff, my parents and Laurie didn't insist. They just kept telling me it was no longer there and they wouldn't bring it back. That is when I could get initiative. I'm not sure but I think I might have tried to drag the table back in there. That sounds like something I might do. When I'm so focused on a compulsion, I can do things I ordinarily can't. I am not even aware I'm doing them. When it is over I'm surprised, also. It was a gradual acceptance of the new room. I worried all morning each time I knew they were going to ask me to go in there. After several trips back and forth to my safe chair and the patience of all who worked with me, I finally relaxed and accepted the new room. It all sounds so silly now.

Debriefing Was Wonderful

The new room was bigger and we could do things there that we couldn't do in the other room. Between Darlene and Dr. Padula, they had all kinds of contraptions for me. Things like walking all different ways on the balance beam – forward, backward, feet crossed and feet uncrossed. It was not easy doing, I tell you. Many times my mind just went blank. Mike got into the act, too, and I think they all had a good time making me miserable. I really tried and they all thought I did a phenomenal job considering my limitations. Praise was always forthcoming but in an adult manner. I started to relax more and looked forward to the sessions. The part I really liked was the debriefings after the physical part was through. I got to tell how I felt about the session. They got a chance to know me as a person. I kind of got a feeling they rather liked the person I was. They took what I said seriously and that meant everything to me.

Anxiety and Frustration at My Meetings

I should mention my involvement in meetings concerning me. I have attended my O.P.S. (Overall Plan of Service) meeting now for four or five years. Maybe I should say attended parts of them. The same old problems kept hampering me. I get overly excited and worried, and then it is in and out time again. Thank goodness, the people there are beginning to understand sensory overload. The first one they even let me chose the room I was most comfortable in. I chose the living room and sat in my rocker. I was fortified with Laurie on one side and Darlene on the other. I had no idea what a O.P.S. meeting was. Sounded pretty scary to me. There were people there I didn't know. They kept me somewhat isolated as they didn't want me to blow it. I was still unpredictable then.

At the first meeting, I remember one incident. They read a list of things you dislike. I guess it is OK if you think that is how you get to know a person. I can think of better ways but that is how things are. Included in the like category were the words "he likes praise." They would stop every once in awhile and ask me if what they were saying was true. I think I shocked them when I said "no" on the word praise. I said I like acknowledgement much better than phony, overdone praise. I hate people going on and on when it is something a person my age should be able to do. It is good to say, "You did well on that and I know it is hard for you." Then leave it alone. Don't tell everyone who comes in how great it was with such overdone enthusiasm. It is embarrassing enough that you can't do it, let alone pointing it out to everyone. Some people might like this, I don't.

I know the forms they use have to satisfy regulations, but the methods they use can be very humiliating. How would you like your most personal flaws flaunted about in a public meeting? "He had three incidents of aggression last quarter." "That was down one from the previous quarter." "Next quarter let's set the goal for two." The person is probably embarrassed that he had any. "Forty-five percent independence on washing his groin, up from thirty-five percent last quarter." How would you like the quality of washing your groin discussed in a meeting with you sitting there? This is especially bad when you can't help yourself anyway.

About the third O.P.S. meeting, an incident happened to me to illustrate this point. I am still humiliated and not sure I want to put this in my book. Things like this can be painful and not easily forgotten. If I leave it in, it will be because I want to help someone else. We were at the part of the meeting were they review your last year's progress or lack of. The report was full of percentages, mostly pla-teaued. Up a few points, down a few points. Sounded like the stock market. People were almost dozing off. This whole thing was really getting to me. Then they started to discuss my toilet-wiping pro-gram. That was the straw that broke the camel's back. Talk about humiliation. There I was, someone who could write letters, poetry etc. and couldn't even wipe his own fanny. Then to have it pointed out in such detail in a public place. I got up and ran out the door with my parents in hot pursuit. They didn't know what was the matter with me. I got almost to the car when Dad caught up with me, letter board in hand. I was too upset to type any message. They finally talked me into coming back inside and setting in my rocking chair. After I rocked a few miles, and I'm sure I made a lot of noise, I was able to talk to my parents and was convinced to come back to the meeting. The meeting had continued throughout this fiasco. I'll bet their mind was really on those percentages. At least, they were wide awake by now. My Mom said to come back and tell them what was the matter. Besides being embarrassed I was starting to get really ticked off. If my Mom knew what I was going to say, she might not have been so eager to get me back. Poor Laurie was nervously FC-ing with me. I told them I didn't have to sit here and listen as to my ability to wipe myself being discussed in public. No one should, no matter how low they thought we were. If I couldn't do it at this age, the agency should provide it as a service. Then I went on to tell them how consumer unfriendly their forms were. They all sat there trying to look not too shocked. No one said anything and I got up and fled to the car. My Dad took me back to the workplace, where I sat in fear the rest of the day. Laurie probably OD'd on mints. In case you are wondering why I can't wipe myself, remember I have no sense of where my body parts are and a distorted sense of being able to feel by touch. God didn't put this part of my body in a very conve-nient place for me. To my amazement, my parents were very pleased with my performance. At least I didn't hit anybody and I was really changing from fight to flight. The staff were talking about revising the whole O.P.S. forms. Hopefully, some good came out of this try-ing incident

Should I Leave My Autistic Comfort Zone?

I was having second thoughts about leaving my autism behind. I knew I was about to make another jump forward, but it is a comforting feeling sometimes to crawl into my autistic shell.

People with autism have a comfort zone of relief we turn to when things get too bad in your world. We also use it to relieve the loneliness and boredom of our existence. We each have made a special place we can go to. It may appear to you that we are in our own little world. You are correct in that assumption. It is a good place to us. You might like this gift sometimes yourself. In fact, it is so pleasurable that we can overuse it. It can become addictive and mesmerizing. People with autism often resent being forced out of this state, especially when they aren't particularly interested in what you want them to do. In fact, I know some autistic people who live almost entirely there. I had noticed the better I was getting, the harder it was becoming to retreat into mine. This scared me a lot. I certainly wasn't ready to face the world yet. I was also afraid I would lose my natural, instinctive qualities of perception as well as my abilities of the psychic nature. This is how I had always moved around in your world. I was really torn as to what direction to take. I was again heading toward my anxious state.

We were due for a Dr. Padula visit. While we were there, a good opportunity came for me to tell him again of my fears. He understood but doubted it would happen. Of course, he had no experience in this line either. He talked on such things as intentionality and purpose. Then said maybe I should talk with Sue. Next time we went to see her I did. We talked a lot about trusting the process, moving from one state to another and growing with each move. She suggested I talk with my spiritual guides about my goals and how to reach them. Also, she said sometimes it is time to leave some things behind. It was up to me to make a move, no one else could do it for me. It was a lonely feeling to be on your own. I resented people always telling me what to do, but now wished someone would step forward. No one did, they just told me it was my decision.

The next few days, at least I think it was – I don't really understand time, I tried contacting my spiritual supporters. Sometimes they are slow coming to the phone. They give you plenty of time to think. When we did make the connection, they said I needed to examine the purpose of my mission, then separate it from my selfish fears and desires. They told me the higher power would not give me any assignment that I couldn't accomplish. They said no one told me it would be easy and help would always be open for me. But as always, they didn't get very concrete. It is always left up to you to find the way. They only provide the support for you to make your own decisions. I know this is the way it must be, though would it be so bad to give me some clues? It is how we grow, however.

Hara Healing

All this was leading up to a Hara Healing. It is an important fact that I was not in my body as a complete person. I was spiritually outside of it much of the time, and could not function efficiently as a person in this world. For many years, I understood what was happening around me but couldn't react because I wasn't whole. This was apparent to Sue right away when she first met me, and this became a goal of ours – to bring my energy inside my body. That was it. This was accomplished every time I met with her, but it would only last a short time. It was not permanent. As I progressed over time, it would last longer, and I was beginning to feel more whole.

Then came the time I was feeling like I might lose some of my special abilities and gifts. Remember, this I had talked over with some of my professionals and they could not assure me it wouldn't happen, even though they thought it unlikely. My whole mission was shaky. Fear was interfering. I was questioning if I was taking on more than I could handle. When I brought this to Sue's attention again, she suggested I might be ready for a Hara Healing. She explained it was to clear the energy pathways and promote intentionality. It was something a little different and by now you know this isn't my bag. The one thing that kept me going was her insistence that I consult my spiritual guides. I did this often as it is just part of my daily life. They didn't promise me anything but gave me more courage to fulfill my mission. They told me again, God would not give me any assignment I couldn't accomplish, but it was up to me to do the work.

On the next visit or two, I talked it over with Sue and she was willing to try. We went up stairs after our usual chat, and I thought I was ready. But when we started the therapy. I became frightened and wanted to stop. She knew it was important that it be my decision and no one else's. I wanted my Mom or Dad to help me and she brought my Mom up to me. Then she assured me that I had done nothing wrong, and if I wanted to try another time, I could. The wonderful thing about Sue was she allowed me to be my own person and never once did I feel any pressure to do otherwise.

It was a miserable failure the first time. Later after several weeks we attempted it again. I was more relaxed and asked her to try. She didn't push me, I asked her. This time it was successful. It helped me regain my confidence in my mission. We do it often now and it is a great experience. It really grounds me. I have not lost my special gifts, but my perception and use of them has changed. They are more connected to reality. I do not live and dwell in them so totally as I once did. Now I am in more control of them and they don't always control me. I can use them in this world as I see the need. I'm sure not perfect yet, and waiver back and forth, but I think I am heading in the right direction.

(Sue – The Japanese use the term "Hara" when referring to the lower belly and the quality and quantity of focus, strength, and energy cultivated in that area. In marital arts it is the center of gravity in the body or the focal point of developed power in which all movement originates.

When we talk about using the Hara in energy work we speak about the intention and purpose to connect with conscious awareness and deep focus into the physical body.

One way Tom has developed the ability to connect more deeply into the body has been with repeated exposure to the energetic, vibrations associated with this grounded nature during our treat-

ments. Like offering a road map to the energy pathways in the body, this exposure has enhanced his understanding of where the boundaries of his body exist in time and space. This is like teaching the dancer how to find the center of power in the body and how to relate that to the dance.)

My Initiative Is Slowly Improving

All of these turmoil experiences seemed to be connected to improvement in my sensory channels. I was getting more initiative all the time. Not in big steps like you might identify with, but baby steps that only those who know me best would notice. I could scratch my itches all the time, and to everyone's disgust I could pick my nose. It felt good to me even though persons with autism are not blessed with many social graces. Darlene and Laurie kept trying to keep me from wiping it on my shirt, but I was getting pretty fast by now. I often see normal people doing it too, but they try to hide it. I still don't know why but since it seems important to you I am trying to be more discreet.

New Glasses Are Hard for Me to Wear

My eyes were really changing now. They seemed to be working together more. I could focus on things a little closer, sometimes but not always. The glasses seemed to make me jumpy. It was a while before it occurred to me that this might be part of the problem. They told me to tell Dr. Padula. I did and he said he would retest my eyes. He did indeed find that I needed a glasses change. I was glad the one lens could be made thinner. It was so thick that it was always popping out of the frame. Of course my sitting on them, stepping on them, and occasionally throwing them didn't help either. We got the new lenses and also got new lighter, more modern-looking frames. I was really excited to get them. Dr. Padula put them on and adjusted them. I had them on a few seconds and guess what, they felt different. The frames didn't feel right. They were so light, I couldn't tell if they were on or not. I didn't like them because they were so different. I saw much differently too. My autistic side hadn't taken this into account. Also, my initiative had improved to the point, I could now take them off and I did. It was weeks before I could wear them consistently. My parents were quite unhappy with me, even though they kept their cool. They kept telling me that it was up to me, but strongly encouraged me to try. Everyone kept telling me how good I looked in them, but that wasn't the problem. They just felt different and my body kept rejecting them. I really had to do a lot of meditating and asking for spiritual help on that one. They had to do some experimenting on the size of the dark tape things on the nose part of the lens. The width of the tape really makes a difference. Even though I wanted control, this was making me decide everything for myself, and beginning to get on my nerves. There are many times I want to go backward and let others make decisions for me.

(Dr. Padula – Following Tom's progress over the course of many months I found that there was improvement over time with his vision, but there were changes in the way in which he attempted to organize his vision at the different stages of neuro-optometric rehabilitation. I found that there was a decline in the visual midline shift syndrome, causing a lesser need for strong prisms to affect his posture and overtime the prism strength would weaken considerably. In addition, Tom began to control his visual processing more effectively by establishing ambient and spatial organization of the focal detail process. This caused him to be able to look at things and people for longer periods of time. This affected his social contacts, as well as his ability to use his eyes to gain information from the world around him. There were times, however, that his visual system seemed to fall back on an old style or habit. This is not unusual for people who are suffering from sever post-trauma vision syndrome. Despite the fact that post trauma vision syndrome produces visual chaos, it is something they are used to. Therefore, the compensation for affecting this old habit will be easier to deal with than the change that is occurring. In Tom's case, there were times when he seemed to regress; however, by re-prescribing prism and/or repositioning binasal occlusion, he was able to lift himself back to the new level quickly.)

New Ways of Learning without Modeling

Meanwhile, back at the workplace, Mike was on his usual monthly visit. He was asking a lot of me now. Real scary stuff! I was finding out my body could do a lot of things that were unbelievable to even me. I was used to modeling movements after someone else. He and Darlene were making me do it on my own. That is incredible work for me. My head hurt from just sorting out my body parts. I had no idea my body had so many parts. I know they often laughed when I yawned in the middle of a hard activity, but it really took it out of me. I was beginning to have a sense of self. I could actually feel my brain working. Confused, sometimes but making progress. This gave me hope and kept me going. I looked forward to these sessions but there was still some dread of failure there. I liked these people and wanted to please them so bad. I was pleased that they seemed thrilled at my progress.

(Mike – Ok, so what have I tried to do? Well for starts I say a man trapped in a body that was not moving enough. He had developed a twisted torsion in the trunk with the right shoulder rotated forward. The posture was accentuated by the fact that Tom is right handed, sits with a slight kyphosis (rounding of the upper trunk) and has been FC-ing a lot. My personal goals were to align the trunk with expansion of the work Darlene had started and make sure that we also gave Tom the postural strength and control to hold any changes in alignment. As we progressed, we also began to see other responses and changes occur. Some were conscious goals of mine and some were not. Tom began to be able to get out of his recliner with less physical prompting. (When I see Tom in his recliner, sometimes it is hard to see where the recliner ends and Tom begins. They blend into each other. This is a safe place for Tom, and I respect it as such.) And, Tom was able to blow out a candle at his mother's birthday.

My service model has primarily been as a secondary to the occupational therapist. The two of us have worked together for many years, and with that in mind, we are able to provide ideas and program suggestions to one another for implementation. This model can be very effective if you have a good working relationship and trust factor with your team members. Trans-disciplinary and inter-disciplinary models are not effective if the team members do not have a trust and confidence in each other's skills. My routine has been to come in approximately one time per month for an hour and conduct a treatment session. Initially, Darlene would observe or co-treat. She would document changes that occurred and progressive activities that were introduced. Tom seemed to always have a special confidence in my ability to get him to expand and perform new movement experiences on the therapy ball, mat, beams or benches. This initial contact with me seemed to then make it possible for Darlene to expand the activities into her more frequent sessions.)

Frustrations with Residential Living

My FC skills were being addressed by now on a regular basis by Laurie, Darlene and my parents. Delicia was my big contact at the residence. Unfortunately, she was only there half the time. The other half had no voice. It is hard for me, who has trouble with flexibility, to adjust to all these different situations. It went from sublime with my folks, to the pits with half of my residential life. Most of the staff still look on us as persons only when it fits their advantage. They don't see it this way, however. It seems to threaten their control, which makes group living harder for them to manage. Unfortunately for us, it makes a regimented life style which we all hate. I long for freedom to go and come as I wish, to eat what I want, and when I want it, some place that has only me to think about. This utopia would have people, who could and would talk to me like you talk to each other. On the other side of the coin, that might be a dull, lonely life without others to watch and hear interact with each other. Unless I get more initiative, and less dependent on others, that is what it would probably turn out to be. Group home living is more exciting. We have to sort this all out soon before I am left on my own. It is my biggest worry.

Dr. Padula Keeps Trying to Expand Horizons

Things keep changing and the cause and effects are always present. Dr. Padula keeps trying to expand the horizons of the known with the unknown. My eyes keep changing too. It is hard to tell if they will ever become normal (as you put it), but they are serving me better for my purposes. Dr. Padula is spending a lot of time picking my brain as to how we, people with autism, perceive the world. He says knowing me and listening to my feedback has changed his way of thinking and perceiving persons with autism a lot. I sincerely hope I am giving him the correct information as the responsibility is quite weighty. I am doing my best and he thinks my perceptions and thoughts are quite plausible and scientifically possible.

We know that I have trouble in integrating an object that I want to see from the background around it. Part of the problem is depth perception, but it is different, I think. It seems to me to be like my hearing difficulties. I have a lot of problems separating background noise from the information I should be paying attention to.

Darlene is usually at our meetings and they are trying to combine movements with visual training. This is done again with a lot of hard work on my part. He is doing things like having me do something up close and at the same time touch something farther away. Also, he is making me use my brain to listen to exact words instead of copying someone else's movements or them pushing my hand. It is very difficult for me to do a command movement and hear exact words at the same time. When I am sorting out my body movements, my hearing suffers. This is a problem I also have with Mike's work. I am improving even though a snail or a turtle would be my timing in your eyes. To me it is a gazelle until I see it on tape. Again, it is when I try to combine sensory channels it becomes a laborious task for me. When no pressure is put on from the outside or inside, my responding processing time is getting near normal most of the time. Another problem, Dr. Padula pointed out, is my inability to follow movement with my eyes first and then follow with a movement of my own. He has been watching me and says most of the time I move first and then try to follow with my eyes. Not very effective or efficient. We are trying very hard to work on that, too. It is difficult for me to think about those things whenever I make a movement. In fact, pretty impossible. I do think about these things sometimes and try to do what he says. When you have forty-some years of patterns, it is hard to change them.

I still need those dark strips on the nose sides of my glasses, which helps my occlusion problems. When they are there, I seem to have more focus ability. They help me concentrate better and bring the world and my problems down to manageable size. We have experimented with adjusting their size and taking them off completely. In a short time, I start becoming anxious and, as I have said before, no one wants to go through any more of my anxiety sessions than necessary. I always end up, so far, putting them back on. I know they make me look different, but I guess I will settle for that at this point in time. Hopefully I can do without them some day.

My glasses have been changed two times now, maybe three. Each time they needed changing, I was having periods of uncertainty and grouchiness and was more obstinate (not my usual adorable self). People, especially my parents, were less patient with my episodes and unreasonable inflexibilities. We would spend a lot of time arguing about issues. I would be told I was unreasonable and stubborn. After a time I could usually see their point. Once in a great while, they would see mine. The gene pool at work. We are a stubborn lot. After the glasses change, things would settle down again. Not immediately; it takes time to adjust. Dr. Padula can tell by the way I use my eyes.

He has somewhat stopped with a lot of the eye exercises. He is more concentrating on what is happening in my developer and how that affects my camera. My eyes keep improving but sometimes I get the feeling he thinks my progress should be better. It could be that I think my progress should be better. It happens so subtly that I have a hard time knowing if I have improved. I **do** know it has, **when** is where I have the trouble.

I do try to use my own eyes when I can, but the habit of using others is well imbedded. Besides, it is kind of fun. My Dad's eyes are the easiest to use, but they aren't as good as they were. I do hope they don't deteriorate anymore or I may have to really use my own or find another pair. Dr. Padula talks of intentionality being a factor and also my problems with inflexibility being based in vision. I am trying to get a better understanding of that concept and how it interfaces with Sue's energy. I know it has a direct connection. If I get an understanding of it, I will write more about it.

Therapeutic Listening Program
(introduced)

I am not sure when the Therapeutic Listening Program started but I think it was about this time. Remember earlier in the book, I was asked about doing Auditory Training and I had said "fix my eyes first,". Well, they got me started in eye training. In the realm of the sensory world/my ears, or hearing, was about the only thing left to work on.

Darlene had gone some place and heard about a program called "Therapeutic Listening." She liked the sound of it and eventually became accredited to supervise it. Soon after Laurie did, also. It is similar but different than Auditory Training. It works on the brain as to modulating sounds and changing hearing patterns. I am not sure if this is correct, someone else needs to explain it better. It is ongoing, unlike Auditory Training, and the CD's are individualized.

You wear headphones and the times are short to begin with. They work the times up to a half-hour, two times a day. They mix and match CD's to your tolerance level. They are special headphones and CD's. I find it very pleasurable and relaxing.

One time they moved me ahead too fast and I got very edgy. They had to back up and take it slower.

There are a list of things that may be signs of improvement. Two things I have noticeably improved on are 1. I now can tell when I am full when eating. 2. I now can follow conversations of others with my head and eyes.

The headphones have been added to my on growing list of things to do each day!

(Darlene – Therapeutic Listening TM uses sound stimulation in combination with sensory integration intervention. Therapeutic Listening TM has been an available intervention tool for occupational therapists and other professionals for the past five years. The training workshop "Listening with the Whole Body" presented by Shelia Frick OTR/L and Colleen Hacker OTRL/L of Therapeutic Resources capitalizes on the use of sound vibration to stimulate brain processing. Therapeutic Listening uses electronically altered compact disks which may vary in the kind of music, the sound quality and the level of activation. A good quality portable CD player and good quality headphones along with the specific CD, based on the individuals needs, can be carried on at home, school or work. This makes sound intervention unique. Each time a CD was added or changed in Tom's sensory diet a probe occurred which was supervised directly by an OT and his parents. First it had to be established that Tom could tolerate the CD selection. Once that occurred the selections addressed his various needs that include: regulation and modulation, spatial temporal organization as it relates to body awareness and balance, postural activation, midline organization, and auditory attention discrimination, and selectivity. The program would be carried out at his residence with data based monitoring by his support staff and monthly monoriting by the OT. Tom's perceptions of the changes and the outcomes of Therapeutic Listening, were observable by many people in his life. He has been a great asset in determining what works and doesn't work for him.)

My Team

I have talked about how my team came together throughout my book. However, I want to emphasize how important this has been. The dynamics of their life changes and how that impacts on mine has to be stressed.

They were all introduced to the team by suggesting each other. Laurie was the only one picked by us (my parents and me). She knew

Darlene from working with her at another place. Darlene knew of Dr. Padula from having contact with him through another client. Dr. Padula knew Sue from having her daughter as a patient. When I needed something more specialized, Darlene brought in Mike. I personally think a higher power was bringing us all together. It is very important that all the members work well together, not only in their disciplines but personalities as well. Our times when we get together are happy ones. Much laughing and some teasing goes on. Positive energy is usually present. They are all open to new ideas. They are all flexible. They did not all come with the same understanding of each other's talents. They varied from solid, substantial Laurie, who has an amazing sense of humor and she has her feet planted firmly in the ground; Darlene blowing in the wind, with great compassion and understanding; Dr. Padula so intuitive and far ahead of his time in his profession; Sue trying to guide us in the energetic, spiritual realm; and Mike so sensitive and in the beginning rather awed by the whole thing. It has been fascinating for me to watch them, change as well as them watching me. When you have as much nonproductive time as I do, you become a big people watcher. They have all changed and learned from each other as well as from me. The important thing is they are willing to change and accept new ideas.

I have grown and changed also, I hope. In the beginning I had little or no experience in interacting with people on a level of this kind. I went from feeling grossly inadequate to "feeling my oats," as you say. Neither is very appropriate. I am very blunt sometimes and don't even know it.

I formed a real attachment to my team as they came into my life. I never had such attention from anyone but my family before. It was exhilarating and almost overwhelming. My autism seems to prevent my relationships from being normal, from your point of view. I get some of the feelings, however. They may be mixed up, to your way of thinking, but they are intense to me.

My first stab at trying to get close to someone who wasn't family was with Laurie. I thought I was in love with her. In my own way, I probably was but not in the sexual sense. I, in a blundering way, told her things like I wanted to come live with her. I did not mean in the usual way. She handled it well but when I knew what everyone thought, I was totally embarrassed. I didn't even want to see her again. She told me it wasn't unusual for a user to become very attached to their facilitator. After a short time everything was OK. Again, a lesson for Tom!

It is important for you to know how events in your close professionals', facilitators' or even caretakers' lives impact on ours. They provide the only chance we have to express ourselves and to feel like real people. When that is threatened, we really panic. We can feel vibrations more definite than you. Also, some of us have experienced loss of people we thought were our friends many times. We know what real hurt is.

Among my professionals and facilitators I have felt when they were drifting away, even though it was temporary. It scares me a lot yet. Two of them have had babies, one got married (I was invited to the wedding this time and had one of the best times of my life).

Sometimes they get involved in other projects. I understand this is normal living but my autistic side panics. I am so afraid of losing my voice (FC voice). I am so dependent on these few. At this point in time, they are my lifeline. I must establish more independence if I am to stop these depressive thoughts. I must be having a bad day as I am usually more upbeat and positive.

I know the novelty of me is wearing off. I miss the excitement of the first meeting. It was new to all of us. Every day was filled with anticipation by me. We were all so close. We still are close but not in the same way. My Mom says that is real life. Sometimes I wonder what I have gotten myself into. I have learned life is a series of ups and downs.

When Sue, my energy therapist got married, I wrote this poem for her. She put it in her wedding program. I had put a lot of thought into it because it was an important step for her.

The Union of Two Special Spirits

I view your love as two separate drops of water
careening down a pane of glass,
making searching, erratic patterns on their way.
Never straight but on course, never predictable
but always bent toward each other.

Finally they touch, making a stronger stream
that becomes more stable, more focused.
Going forward to join others,
always forward joining others.

It gains strength and satisfaction
as its outreach touches beyond its scope.
Its stability produces satisfaction and joy
to all who care, to all who care about mankind.

My Body Has a Mind of Its Own

I know I have gotten better in many ways but sometimes a change in my routine can trigger a setback. I know they are all part of my same autistic problem. Even recently this popped up again. A while back we had used the video technique as a training tool at the workplace. Since it was done with the same people and at the same time no problems occurred. It was proving to be a successful tool. Mike, Darlene and I decided that my physical therapy should become part of my group home staff's responsibility. Sounds logical. Again great arrangements were underway. We decided another video for the home would be the best training tool. Now, the only problem was how to get it done. I was consulted but I didn't know how to break my inflexible routined schedule either. My mind is clear on what I should do but my confounded body won't accept new orders. It's like a computer without a proper programmer. My screen (body) just comes up with "Can not process this request."

The big day arrived (or should I say the big late afternoon). Another change, all my sessions with Mike were earlier in the day. Alison, a staff member, had gone to great deal of trouble moving mats, lights, TV, etc. to the basement. I could hear her down there and it made me anxious. When things are too set up, it is just as bad as no preparations at all. The vibes are what count and that is hard or often impossible to control. They were pretty prevalent here. Everyone did their part well, like in a play, but that negative energy was all over the place.

Mike came (to my body, he wasn't supposed to be **there** at that **time**). Again my mind was clear but my body won! It got up and ran to the door, but my Mom was blocking it. I tried pushing her away. She is pretty game for a little person and stuck her ground. Unfortunately, I am a bigger person and could have swatted her but I don't do those things anymore. My mind took me back to my chair. Then my body took me back to the door and then eventually to an alternative route through the basement (I'm getting smarter). You can't imagine the turmoil of mind and body fighting like this. Then the sensory system goes haywire. At some point I ended up sitting in our car. Stuck as if with Crazy Glue.

They let me sit for awhile, as they plotted their course of action. Once I get settled in like that, it is impossible for me to move or someone else to move me. Eventually Mom came out to plead her case. She told me all the reasons I should come in and they only expected me to do a couple of things. My body said, "No way Jose." Then Mike came out and told me I shouldn't be discouraged. He said if I couldn't do it this way, we would find another. He was so patient and understanding. They, (he and my Mom) said they had taken things too fast. To many changes all at once. Those were the sweetest words I ever heard. My body began to relax and I regained my senses little by little. I just wanted to get back into my time frame and routine. Dad came to the car and we started into my nightly routine.

Mom and the rest talked about how we could do it better. In my feedback, in the car, I told them I was frightened of the basement and didn't want to go down there. It is a typical basement, dark and dingy. The energy is not positive. We decided to do it upstairs, which required moving some furniture. The whole process required changing things around my idiosyncrasies. I feel bad about this, but it all depends on whether you want this to succeed. From your normal prospective, it sounds like I am a spoiled brat, but if you could see my shaking hands and anxious facade, you would know it is real.

Cutting to the chase, it took several visits to the house by Mike, changing the time of day to morning (breaking my routined morning patterns), training and introducing each staff member individually, and my accepting them. I especially want to recognize Delicia, my main link to my home at Opportunity House. She is able to truly get in my head and know what I am thinking. If it wasn't for her, I might still be standing at the door. I want to give credit to Doug and most of the staff for they try hard to satisfy my needs.

Now it is going well, but what a difficult task to get such a seemingly easy job done. I really get discouraged sometimes with my body with such a mind of its own. It is coming around but on some occasions like this, it can cause a real tussle. I hope my team will stick with me until I can better assume control.

(Mike – As time passed, Tom's needs changed and there was a need to make the ball activities occur frequently. Tom selected a staff member at his work site that he felt confident with to carry out the program on a daily or at least a few times per week basis. With all good plans the person selected only stayed on the job for a short period of time following the training (picture-based instruction and one-on-one training). The ball program went to the side with people in Tom's life other than Darlene and myself. I have always taken my lead from Tom regarding how and when to introduce changes in his daily routines. When he is ready, he has always let me know. Last year upon Tom's suggestion we made a video workout tape. It was a tape of Tom and myself performing activities that we felt he could do with coaching and set up from work site staff. Darlene videotaped the session (20 minutes) and then trained the staff on how to coach Tom through it. I feel that one of the best parts of the videotaped program is that Tom was able to hear my voice and cues to perform the tasks. Some of the tasks were simple for Tom in a one-on-one

session with me, however the same activity with a different person takes on a whole host of new challenges for Tom. The videotape was very successful and was able to be progressed in only a few months. But as with all things in life, staff changed, routines changed and the second tape was kept in place for a longer period of time to allow for consistent usage. The positive piece is that it means that Tom had to use the tape with a greater variety of people.

As the frequency of the videotape programming decreased at the work site, Tom suggested we do a second tape at his home. This was going to be very challenging for a variety of reasons. The first is seeing me at a different time of day. He was used to seeing me at 10:00 a.m. Now I would be coming to his home at the end of the day, 4:00 p.m. The first time going to the house was quite a scene. The whole gang was coming, Mom, Dad, the house manager, house staff, Darlene and myself. I had never been to the house before, but I was told that there was a good location in the basement where other exercise equipment was used by Tom's housemates. A space with a mat and Tom's ball would be set up there. Well, to cut to the chase, Tom had not been in the basement very often at that time of day, which was associated with other routines that were strongly rooted for 18 years. Nothing got physically accomplished. Tom bolted out of the house twice and was very unnerved, and he was feeling that he failed. Of course he did not fail. It was just a stepping stone. Emotionally I felt it was great. Tom and I needed to have this crazy experience to let us both know that we needed to change some of the variables in the scene and try again. We persevered since it was a goal of Tom's to make it happen no matter how difficult it was for him. He is now using a videotaped exercise program in the home at 9:00 a.m. with expanded training to new staff.)

Inflexible

If I could have a wish.
I know what it would be.
To be able to move my body
as others freely do.

It stops moving and gets stuck
like putting it in neutral,
pushing on the gas, and
wondering why it won't go.

Then confusion takes over
and the problem gets worse
 until it consumes me and I am lost.

I hear what you are saying
and I truly want to move
but my body will not react.

Sometimes a touch will
break the cycle and
sometimes waiting will help.

Please take this time to help me,
as I am in deep trouble.
I am not in control, so be patient.

Eventually my head will clear
and I will be the same Tom again.
I think you call it inflexible,
but I call it hell!

Energy and Me at the Present Time

As I have stated in other parts of my book, it is difficult to separate what is causing my improvements. All of the therapies contribute on their own merit, but also integrate into each others as well. Energy therapy probably does this more than most. It has helped me better understand myself and gain more control of my actions. I have learned to meditate and put perspective on my spiritual beliefs. My beliefs have become more focused and my mission better defined.

I no longer think in terms of myself only. My concept of time is slowly taking form thus increasing my flexibility. I can think things through more thoroughly. Most of the time I can get and keep my senses together enough to keep me from going completely out of control. I still have a long way to go, but I am off and running.

In each of my sessions with Sue, we start by just talking. She lets me tell her anything I want and as long as I want. She helped me put together my own thoughts and feelings. They are definitely <u>my own</u> thoughts and feelings. She makes me think and put together my own solutions, and she challenges me big time and is always pushing me to reach for higher horizons (sometimes I don't appreciate it at the moment). I truly respect her opinions and the way she interacts with me. I think she knows and understands me best. Her therapy is with me all the time in all I do. Sue and her energy are truly the glue that holds me together.

(Sue – For Tom, the work has meant the opportunity to more fully enter into the physical body. His new found ability to make better sense of multisensory input has helped him adapt to his environment. He enjoys increased motor mobility and dramatically increased initiating skills that allow the freedom of choice in almost any given situation. He has a greatly enhanced ability to stay present even in energetically threatening environments. He is becoming spontaneous and his physical affect and facial expressions now often reflect his feelings.

His emotional body has expanded allowing the information response time to increase, thus creating the ability to relate in more purposeful and caring ways to self and others. The outbursts of an-

nihilating anger and self-injurious behaviors have nearly ceased.

On the mental level he is participating in key decision making processes that reflect his desire to create his life the way he wants. He contributes brilliant analogies of energetic and spiritual interpretations of the worlds in which we live.

Spiritually, he carries a message worth listening to. A missing link for many. We are far more than we can see. He teaches us that the unfamiliar costume he wears is not who he is at all and that beyond the physical body lies a vast world of experiences just waiting for our exploration. It challenges us to reflect on the accuracy of our interpretation of what it means to think, feel and to know. It invites us to see that even though he is from a group that often lives on the fringes of society, that he is no less competent, but is in fact highly gifted.

I've heard that the autistic call themselves the Freedom Fighters. Who's freedom are they fighting for ours or theirs?)

Physical Therapy Is Progressing

My work with Mike is really taking off. He is expecting me to work more things out on my own and stick with them for long periods of time. He is really pushing my limits. I am not only doing therapy ball exercises but am now doing pulling exercises from some contraption they have rigged up on the therapy swing pulley. They have continued and expanded the work on the balance boards. They took a video quite a while ago (I think), to be used as a training device for the staff. I saw it and was pleased to have the staff able to see some of the obvious (to my team) problems. Darlene could point them out and explain them. The staff seemed really interested for the first time and acted like they wanted to get involved. They took another one recently and I had improved drastically. Viola! Before and after videos – the wonders of technology. I viewed them with my parents and really had ambivalent feelings. It is hard to watch yourself look so pathetically bad. So bad the viewers are straining to help you out – like opening your mouth when you want a baby to take a bite of food. Also in the second one I am making noises and totally unaware I am doing it. It is really embarrassing. I am glad from the standpoint I am helping others. That overrides the embarrassment. I am impressed with myself from that standpoint. A different Tom from the poor, ole, failure Tom of before. I have finished my third video and am doing a lot better. I'm sure no Olympic hopeful but satisfying myself is twice as sweet. A long way to go but a start.

The staff needs to know, they won't be as successful as Mike. Yet, much of my success comes from his confidence in me and my confidence in him. There is an energetic connection there. This has to be built with each person. There must be commitment and caring and out of this comes trust. It is a long road but if you stick with it, it can be worth it. At least for me.

Mike is now trying to FC with me with varying results. He gets a word now and then and sometimes a phrase. He is not sure why we couldn't get it perfect right off. We have the relationship and trust already built in. He asked me the if I knew why we were having trouble. I told him it was because he was scared. He said, "Not really," I said that he does not have the confidence that he has when we are in his world of physical therapy. Therefore, our relationship is changed. I don't feel his strength of confidence and our relationship is different. We will get it, though, because he wants it and will keep pursuing.

At This Moment – My Feelings about FC and Independence

My abilities of independence with FC varies from day to day, sometimes from hour to hour, even minute to minute. It certainly has a lot to do with my sensory system which certainly affects my anxiety level or vice-versa. All of that impacts on both energy levels (user and facilitator).

I now have extremes from hand support to a hand on the elbow for just a short time. The latter is when I have just received some strong sensory input such as a hand massage and joint compression.

Then, for a short time, I am much more aware of where my hands and fingers are. Laurie is really working hard on this for me. On rare occasions I can almost do it by myself with just a slight touch on my wrist. After a few lines, I become very inaccurate. It is very difficult to read and it takes a real pro to decipher it. We have an Intellikeys Keyboard for my computer. My Dad made a key guard for it so I have to be more accurate in my touch. This is very tiring for both my eyes and controlling my movements. Delicia, my lifeline at my group home residence, is working hard to help me achieve this goal of independence.

It sounds like my FC abilities are nearly at a standstill. At this time, they are different with each facilitator. For those few, like my parents, I rarely put in spaces between words and use proper punctuation. They are so good at reading my FC typing and can do it very fast. That is called "poor practice" and certainly not approved of in FC circles but I love it. It cuts to the chase! Think about how it must feel to have to type out each letter for every thought in your head. You might look for short cuts, also. Those who use sign language do it, I think they call it "amslam." Of course, we are not allowed to even think of such a thing. It is too bad not to be allowed to be normal when that is what you are insisting we become. No wonder we are confused. I think so much faster than I can produce that it's sometimes hard to integrate the two.

When I know someone is just beginning, or someone is going to be strict, like Laurie, or someone just doesn't have the skills, I can shape up. I know how to use the space bar and can punctuate fairly well. I do it when called for. I am talking about typing on the letterboard. When I use the computer, I have to do it correctly. I prefer the letterboard for selfish reasons. It is more convenient, portable and faster for my ultimate purposes, talking to you. At that time, I really don't care what you think. I just want to express myself!

Sometimes I wonder if my whole heart is really into becoming totally independent. My social life is almost all built around my ability to facilitate. When I FC someone has to be close to me and for that time we are very much in social contact. I like that! Would that stay the same if I became independent? I have grown to enjoy the social

106

aspect of this and can't possibly imagine life without it now. It is what I live for. I had 36 years without social contact before. Most people, even now, only interact with me to find out something. I have such initiation problems and if that doesn't improve drastically, I wouldn't be able to type on my own anyway. I see others in the same situation. I realize that it might be replaced by something that you think is better. I am not sure if I would like it!

On the other hand, if I don't make it to independence, a large number of people won't ever believe it is me. That is very important if I am ever to get my messages out and accomplish my mission in life.

I know a lot of authorities in FC are very concerned with this aspect. They are having trouble being believed, also. Their professional careers are at stake, but you can't make people like me completely independent if our sensory systems are so fragile and askew. That has to be cleared up first. Since that is different in each one of us, the degree of attained independence will be different, too. I really appreciate Laurie's willingness to stick her neck out for me. Her professionalism is on the line, I know! I really want both independence and the social part desperately.

I know I will not always have someone with me who can facilitate. I really want to talk. Laurie says the motor part of my talking is a movement disorder. I hope I can overcome this. We will see if it is in God's plan. Right now the words are stuck in my throat.

I don't know myself how the energy factor would be affected. I have heard of a lot of cases where a user becomes independent but can't type if their facilitator is not in the room. It sounds to me like they are still attached by an energetic connection. I think I am still attached to facilitators in this way, also.

Again, I am scared. I am very needy in a lot of areas!

(Laurie – When typing on a P.C. Tom uses an Intellikeys Keyboard with a key guard. This is an expanded keyboard that can be used instead of a traditional one. Because of its large size, each key is a slightly bigger target for Tom to hit. The key guard prevents Tom's finger from slipping off a key or hitting two keys at one time. By using the Intellikey Keyboard Tom's precision of typing increases.)

My Closing Thoughts

My life has really changed a great deal. I am still autistic and fight the problems daily. I hope some day to conquer the part that keeps me from participating and doing the things I want to do, but I'm happier now with my life. The quality has changed immensely and today my life has meaning. I have goals and happy moments that a few years ago were not even in my imagination. I am consulted on my challenging problems and many times I'm able to make suggestions that work. When I can't, I have a better understanding when people try to help me solve my problems. It is not all roses yet, some of the thorns still stick out. But what wonderful progress to have input into the solutions of your challenges. My life is more in my hands and the responsibility leads to more commitment from me.

We must look at what each individual wants from life and my quality choices may not be everyone's. We are all individuals with different systems. There is no one roadmap. Everyone needs to be analyzed to their variations. Then find and fund the available supports. We want to interact but only on the terms that our sensory systems will allow.

I think motivating the person with autism is the most important single factor in working with them. If this desire isn't there you are in a mode of eternal failure. Would you climb a mountain to win a race if it meant nothing to you? I don't think so. We are asked to climb mountains all the time without a good reason to get to the top. Motivation must be continuous and include long- and short-term incentives. For me real work and not fake is very important and motivating. I must be doing as much of it as I can with the thought that I can eventually do more. Don't lie to me but push me within my capabilities.

This is why communication is so critical. The clients and the people they interact with must learn to read one another. All people throw off vibrations that many people with autism can feel. In the beginning it is about the only thing we have going for us and we develop this skill to a high degree. I still have this ability and depend on it largely.

I think horses and horse whisperer people communicate this way. If they can do it why can't we? Persons with autism are reading you every moment but few people are reading them. Just imagine trying to communicate with someone and having them ignore you.

I am only considered disabled by people who can't get beyond the outward signs of autism and into my head and feelings. That can be difficult but the reward will be to find a person who is ready to relate and share the joys and sadness of life with you.

A More Satisfied Soul

(A Sequel to the Poem, The Two Me's, page 11)

The two me's are slowly blending into one.
A long process has finally begun.
I am gaining the sought-after power I need.
I must tame this monster to succeed.

To do this you must have a strong desire.
Without it you will most certainly tire.
Desire I had and motivation it became.
Once that happened I was in the game.

I still feel rage and anxious I get.
It's impossible to never be upset.
I've found it is possible to stay in control,
but it certainly plays havoc with my soul.

My mind says one thing and my body says no.
In my brain a tussle, then here we go.
Now my mind has started to usually win.
Before, my body always committed the sin.

You can't believe the concentration it takes.
Sometimes inside and out I really do quake.
For me this still can be quite scary.
From the vibrations I feel some are still wary.

It is worth the pain and frustration I feel
not to have the remorse that was so real.
I get such a high just to know I am winning.
My face may not show it but inside I am grinning.

I've made a pledge never more to aggress.
I've had years of experience with the other mess.
I pray God will help me live up to this goal.
In the hereafter I will have a more satisfied soul.

Tom Page – May 2002

Musings from Mom

Tom has mentioned motivation many times in his book. I would like to expand on the subject a little. In order to motivate the person with autism you must be motivated yourself. This may not be easy especially when the person is no longer a child and many treatments, techniques, programs have been tried and failed over a period of years. We certainly fell in this category.

You must get in an open, positive frame of mind and truly feel all things are possible. Notice, I did not say a gullible frame of mind, especially when using the FC method. There is a difference! If you are using this method there are many people out there who will tell you that you are so needy for this communication that the whole FC concept is a hoax. This is hard to take and you will be put to the test.

Your expectations are necessary and acceptance is crucial. The person (user) comes to the situation very fearful and most always with an extremely fragile system. They are very aware of your feelings and instead of trying to hide them, discuss them with the person. It is OK to tell them you are also fearful, uncomfortable, etc., but reinforce it with "I care enough to try to overcome it and we will work through it!" They will respect you for this. Your relationship with them is critical!

As Tom has said in his book, I am naturally a very skeptical person and this whole thing was totally out of my realm. The turning point.

for me, in becoming a "believer" was when he told me some things I didn't know or expect and found out later he was right. I have turned from a very conservative, traditional person to more "far out" than I thought possible. Frankly, I like it out here better.

I have heard and read, from the opposition, about the FC method being put into practice with just a day or two of instruction. That may happen to a few but in my experience it is a much more complex process than that. With my husband, it took the better part of a year to become conversational. Most people who fail do not stick with it long enough or are themselves not motivated or confident enough to give the users the **confidence they need.** I want to say right here that I don't believe the FC approach is right for everyone but I surely think it is worth a good hard try!

I have led a FC group for four years. It is composed of nine users. It had a shaky beginning and believe me I was fearful and not confident. The users really now look forward to the bimonthly meetings. We have a variety of discussion topics ranging from currents events and learning about autism (one of their favorites) to having speakers, etc. All on an adult level. All the group tell how much they love their parents and, interestingly, about half express sadness that one or both of their parents do not believe they are smart or want to really talk to them. I am at a loss how to help them!

So far, I have only talked about using the FC method. It in itself is not the total answer but only the start of a chain of events. In our case, it provided the realization that our son might not be retarded. This was a turning point in our becoming motivated to motivate him to improve. The more conversational we became with him, the more we learned **from** him. It soon became evident **he** had the key to his own improvement. At that point we decided to try to provide him with the necessary supports needed to help his sensitive system. The cost factor would have to be not an issue (within reason, of course). Naturally, we showered him with individual attention (in a different, more adult way). He became included in most of our conversation when he was with us. A very important point—they need to feel like they are an important contributing member of your family or group.

Not just someone who makes choices or tells you their needs. It must go beyond that. This takes time and patience allowing them to move at **their** own pace The hard part is relinquishing your control and little by little letting them assume as much responsibility for their lives as they can handle, gently insisting they need to do so and convincing them they can do it even with the difficulties they have. A lot of talking to them about this must happen on your part. If they don't become motivated to help themselves, I don't believe it will happen! You talk and listen and try to supply the supports! Not an easy task. It has and will continue to take years for us!

The rewards, for us, have been worth it despite the negative energy from the outside. Frankly, I really don't care anymore except if it hurts Tom. He is really pretty "cool" about it and says, " It is all part of the process." We have plenty of friends and believers who know us and the situation. When I see him do complicated tasks that require motor planning such as cutting meat, carrying several objects at one time, shifting things from hand to hand automatically, something is working. He has not had an incident of aggression for over four years. Short periods of anxiety, yes but now he is able to talk about it and clear up the matter. Usually it takes 10 to15 minutes; it used to take days. He now attends church and other events regularly. If he knows in advance he must be very quiet, he usually can get his noises under control. Still sometimes he has trouble but can tell you he just can't do it today. We always respect his judgement (only he knows). His processing time is near normal most of the time. At times his sensory system still interferes and he doesn't fully comprehend the situation. This contributes to periods of inflexibility, etc., but what an improvement. He now spends a lot of time out in the community with staff as well as us. Most of his staff never knew the old Tom and can't imagine what his past had been. For me, the best part is being able to relax when we are out or he is out with staff and not worry about what will happen. He is truly a different person, yet a long way to go but gaining everyday. Can't argue with these life-altering successes.

Would we do it again? Yes indeed! Everyone's situation is different and each family must chose the course of treatment for themselves.

The course we have chosen is not an easy one. There certainly are times when we wonder what we have gotten ourselves into. A well rounded family we are not. We do have other interests, however. This course is one which takes long-term commitment. It is not fair to the person with autism to tease them with partial involvement.

We know where we have been, where we are now, but the future is still out there. The unknown is, as always, unknown. At the present we are working to provide supports he will need when we are no longer around. We can only continue to "trust the process."

PART 4
Special Stories

Sally's Story:
Relationship Changes with My Sister

At some point, I really began thinking about relationships and how they affect my life. That doesn't seem to follow what autism is all about. We aren't supposed to have those feelings about others, only ourselves. It may be my own personal evaluation or we may all have it deep inside. My feelings about this really began to bug me. My relationship with my sister was bothering me a lot. When we were young, she and I were as close as an autistic person and their siblings could be. She let

me share her life and her friends. I was allowed to rock on her bed to the beat of Herman's Hermits, The Hollies, etc. I was invited in by her when my parents had to knock and hope for permission to enter her inner-sanctum; teenage stage of life must really be difficult. I was always tolerated at her slumber parties. I interacted, even though at a distance with the neighborhood kids, playing with my everpresent ping pong balls near their games and other play. They befriended me against others who came into our domain. I was very lucky in this respect. My parents did well by me then. My sister was super, and nearly all our neighbors treated me well.

As a teenager, I became an elephant and at times became vicious; I could feel my sister and my relationship being strained. By that time I could hurt. I could feel her hurt and anger at me. When you are that age you don't understand many things. She became resentful after having treated me so well. I could feel this and it made me worse. Before long she was the one I would hit before anyone else. She thought it was because I didn't like her, but in reality it was because I really did like her. I was scared I was losing her affection. I was losing more control all the time any way. It became a vicious cycle. None of us understood what was happening. My parents intervened when ever they could. It was a scary time in our lives. I remember a lot of tears, and talk about how much a family could take. I never once, however, heard them say they would send me away. I could feel my Mom worrying that it might come to that. My sister was becoming scared of me and for good reasons. I was scared too and the more scared I became the worse I treated her. I had no voice then and couldn't even talk it out. To make matters worse we moved to Connecticut, and within a year she left for college. I don't want you to think there were daily battles, just enough to make living uneasy. When she went away, I don't remember anyone telling me where she was going or why. I thought for years she left because of me. I had driven her away. It made me so bitter, that I began to blame her for not caring enough for me to want to repair the damage. It wasn't a good situation. At that time, nobody had any idea of my abilities, including my emotions. Inside, I was a wreck. Outside, I was a real jerk. That was all they could see.

(Mom – Tom has said several times in the book that he doesn't remember us talking to him about important events in his life. In defense, I'm sure things were discussed around him and he was included within our family circle. As he says, none of us, including him, had any understanding of his potential. Therefore, I'm sure it was not presented in such adult detail as it is now).

I was becoming a teenager, too. I already had enough turmoil within me, but add teenage hormones and you really have a problem. It certainly didn't get better after we made the move. I only saw Sally a few times during her college years along with summers. There were good times and tense times. We tried hard to be a close family, but things had changed. Things change in ordinary families, too, but I missed the stability I once had and did my part to create a climate where it wasn't going to get any better. Sally always said I knew what she was thinking and also said she didn't appreciate it. We used to spend time just looking at each other from a distance. I must say things weren't as bad as this sounds. We did have a life and I'm only talking about underlying feelings. No one was desperately unhappy, just these things were in our feelings. We continued to take our vacations and go about our life pattern. We just bit the bullet and toughed it out.

Sally Comes Back from College to Live

When her college years were over, she came back home to live. From what I heard, she had to make a choice between a car and an apartment. She chose the car and that meant living home for awhile as she was teaching nearby. I still thought she didn't like me and thought of me as an interferor in her life. After all, she got a taste of what life was like without me. She had boyfriends that came and went all through high school and college. My parents always tried to plan my activities to be sure I had all my clothes on and was as normal as they could make me when her boyfriends came. Not an easy task! She and I ignored each other a lot. I know she was probably jealous of the attention my parents had to spend on me. It was a tough situation for everyone. I still didn't understand it and resented her change. She made overtures to be nice to me, and I'm sure I rejected them. I was hurt as well as she.

I Missed Sally's Wedding

In a few years she met and married her husband. I was not invited to the wedding. They tell me now they went back and forth about it. I was really unpredictable about then, and when sensory overload took over, could become quite aggressive. I don't blame them, but I still can't look at the wedding pictures. I truly wanted to be acceptable but had no control at all. I don't blame anybody but it still hurts.

After they were married she moved out. I went to visit often with my parents. They continued to live not far away. Our relationship became more distant. She no longer sat with me when my folks went out. She was always nice to me and accepted me as I was, but I could feel the wall between us growing thicker. I think she was frustrated about it, but circumstances dictated what was happening. I don't think her husband trusted me either. I'm sure the stories he heard helped shape his opinion. If you haven't grown up with this situation, it must be pretty strange. He witnessed a few episodes that put him in a protective mode. During this time, I was not as aware of what was actually happening. It has only been later that I put this scenario together. I only felt pain, confusion and hurt. My response to this was rebellion. It manifested itself in unpredictability, everyone being uneasy and I felt awful. It was about this time I moved into the group home. That is a whole other story, which I will tell about later. I could lose control easily and was angry at myself too. Again not every minute was like this, but my memories are vivid and sometimes override the good.

I Become an Uncle for Three

She then had children. Everyone was worried of my reaction to them. Many times people with autism don't care for children and animals. They both have unpredictable movements and noises. This throws us into a state of panic. We need routine and structured predictability to keep us calm both inside and out. Most people with autism usually go into their own world when either are threatened. When this doesn't happen you've got trouble. Of course this wasn't known at that time. When the kids were small and they got anywhere near me I could feel the blockade, no matter how discreet they tried to be. It was uncomfortable for me too. I was angry at myself for lack of control, and I was angry at them for no trust. Talk about self-fulfilling prophecy. This was the perfect setup . Luckily, though, I never did hurt them, ever! I really put forth every effort possible not to. I really liked them. They were so cute and interesting to watch. They liked me too, and used to bring me all my favorite things and pile them over me. They accepted me like I was, then. They looked at me sometimes when I made noises, especially after they learned to talk a little, but I was just considered unusual. No big deal to them.

They moved to Michigan when the kids were small. This meant we didn't see them as often. As they grew, Sally must have done a good job of explaining the questions about me, because I always felt accepted by them. Though I felt Sally and my relationship was bad as ever. All of this was before FC. Even with my unpredictable behavior, we made the trip to Michigan and back and hoped for the best. I did put forth as much effort in control as I could then, and we did not have any major incidents.

FC Brings Complications

About this time I really started to think a lot more on my own. The relationship with her was becoming a priority. My new-found ability to FC was not as thrilling to her as I had hoped. She was very skeptical. I can understand why. She, like many others, knew the pitfalls of parent reaction to new theories. It is hard to be a parent and not wish for miracles, even skeptical types like my Mom. Everyone wants to talk to their person with autism, therefore it is assumed by many that this is a fake. It is them doing the talking through our fingers. This is hard to fight especially without a lot of scientific reasons for it to be happening. I am sure Sally is one of these. In fact, if she fell right in line, I would have been more suspicious. She didn't talk negative about it, just didn't talk. I could feel her vibrations and didn't know what to do. We were all frustrated.

I'm sure she must have thought about the impact on both her and my life if this were true. She really cared about me as well as my parents. What to do about me when my parents could no longer be responsible? This was always on everyone's mind except mine when I was younger. It really hadn't been a worry to me, until I started putting things together. I do remember her telling my Mom she would come over here occasionally to see I was taken care of. What good would that be if she was still scared of me? I'm sure she wasn't sure how that would work out either but truly wanted to do what she could and should. Unfortunately, there is no good solution to this problem. This might be acceptable if I was retarded in the sense that I didn't have feelings and all other things people with autism are supposed to come with. In her wanting to care for me, it put a whole new light on the matter. Now I might be a person in every sense of the word. This is different than only seeing to my physical needs. Responsibility in a totally different sense. One that she may not be able to do. I truly feel sorry for her. She must have been torn and ambivalent. Add that to a couple of negative TV shows, and it is a wonder we ever got on any track again. This could certainly complicate her life. She is a good person and I'm sure she was frustrated with the possible new information. She half-heartedly acted enthused.

I wasn't sure what to do about it. I didn't know if anything could be done about it. You can't make a person feel or believe things. In fact it could make things worse. You could tell she didn't want to discuss it. She is like my Dad and keeps things inside. I think I am more like my Mom and tell more than anyone wants to know. I'm not at all sure which is the best. We went on like this for sometime. At least, it seemed like what you say is "sometime." I kept trying to think of a way to help. Finally I came up with one.

Reaching Out to Sally

My parents were shocked one day when I told them I wanted to buy Sally something. I asked them if I had any money. I had no idea as no one ever discussed this with me. My needs had always just appeared. They said I did have some and wanted to know why I asked. I said I wanted to buy Sally a present with my own money. I knew we were going out to see her soon. They said I could and we discussed what she might like. My Mom gave several suggestions and I picked earrings. I know Sally is picky so we decided to let her pick out her own and I pay for them. I was excited about this but scared too. What if she rejected me, even in the slightest way, I would be able to feel it!

We didn't make the trip right away and I was becoming very nervous about it. Knowing me, that is not a good thing. It is hard to find time alone with her when there are three little kids running around. Finally, my Mom said I had something to tell her and we all took our usual places for a talk. She dutifully sat down to listen. Tact not being one of my strong points, I hastily said, "I want to buy you a present with my own money." She just stared at me and said something like, "You don't have to do that." I said, "Yes I did." She probably got "the look" from my Mom and didn't protest anymore. I was puzzled. I told her I wanted to buy her some earrings but wanted her to pick them out. She is allergic to cheap ones, I had heard her talk about that. So they had to be good ones.

Such preparations for this momentous occasion. We were all nervous how this would all play out. Plans were made to go to the department store in the mall. When we got there I got cold feet and couldn't get myself in the store. We finally decided to sit on the bench in front of the store, my Dad, myself and three grandkids. My Mom and Sally went in to pick out the earrings. You don't know Sally, but she has to look at every pair in the store, at least once. A shop till you drop, she is. We picked a place to sit where we could watch her. When she finally settled on a pair, she came out and it was my time to perform. I was scared to death, but Dad handed me the money, which I couldn't feel. I remember my Mom wrapping my fingers around it. Sally, Mom and I marched into the sales lady. Sally did the talking and I handed her the money. It doesn't sound like much but it was one of my proudest moments, and a seed for a new relationship was planted.

It Is Respect for One Another That Counts

I think my sister was really got. She was a believer for a short time anyway. I'm sure she used to go back and forth with this dilemma and without the stimulus of our constant presence, usually turned negative. In fact it still happens, I can feel it. I can't blame her as she doesn't have the kind of support on her end to reinforce it. Then, when I get into some of my mystical side, she truly doesn't understand at all. This goes against a lot of her beliefs and the majority of her acquaintances are of like kind. That is where she is in life and this is where I am. <u>We neither have to give up this aspect of ourselves to have a relationship, but we only have to respect each other's differences.</u> Hopefully that is what is happening now.

Complications of Testing

After the earring experience, my parents thought maybe our exchanging letters would help. She was cooperative and polite. Then she did what all skeptical people do, ask about some specific detail that only she and I would know. That puts unbelievable pressure on us and we usually can't stand up to it. It is something like some of you can't take tests. I've heard people say when they first look at it, they can't remember anything. It is only when they begin to settle down that it begins to make sense. Our trouble is much more intense, only we don't usually get a chance to settle down and then be asked again. You call it being psyched out. We are so psyched out all the time that messages don't even get through. We get tested like we don't have any feelings of that kind. It doesn't make much difference how many times we are exposed to an environment as much as how we feel inside that day, and you can't always see that. Getting used to the same environment helps but it is not the end all. Test all you want but you will be confused and many times disappointed. Doesn't the change in life action and all that goes with it count for more than your scientific jargon? It sure does to us! Unfortunately we are putty in your hands. I am no longer willing to lay there until you mold me. I am going to take shape with or without your help. Frightening isn't it?

Sally and I Are Getting Closer

Meanwhile back to Sally and the letter writing. The first ones my Mom FCed with me. This went on for awhile and then our letter writing dropped off. I still don't know if she believed it was my thoughts or Mom's. I knew this and suggested maybe Laurie help me write the letters. I thought Sally might be more comfortable with this method. We did this so we could talk freely without Mom being involved. It worked for awhile then dropped off again.

We have come a long way since then. Now we talk with the help of a speaker phone. It takes time for my parents to assist me with the FC part, but phone companies are probably happy. I feel that she and I are becoming closer. Hopefully, my vibes are on the money this time. She still doesn't understand me, but she has not had the opportunity that people close to me have had to interact with me often since I learned to FC.

Her family has really changed in the way they treat me. They were always nice but now I'm treated as a grown person. It shows in the gifts they buy me and the places they take me when I visit them. I feel they love and care about me. It isn't perfect yet but Rome wasn't built in a day. Sally has been a good sister and mother. She has done this over long distance and operated under tough circumstances. A mother has a lot of responsibilities, add to that a handicapped brother and she is doing pretty well. I appreciate them all for their efforts.

Our birthdays are only two days apart.

A Birthday Poem for Sally

Our birthdays are almost here.
We are approaching middle age, my dear.
You will always be older, by five,
Guess we should just be glad we're alive.

You were my idol when we were young,
On my ladder, the very top rung.
You shielded me from life's blows,
I showed you very little, I know.
To make it up now is my dream,

I know it is to be in life's scheme.
I will do my part if I can,
Must be soon,
I'm a middle age man.

(Sally – I am very proud of Tommy. As he says in this chapter, my memories of him are mostly as a young child and teenager. Now I see him two or three times a year. He is very dedicated towards his mission of teaching people about autism. He is a goodhearted and kind person who only wants the best for everyone. We have had some uncomfortable times in the past few years because I am not around him long enough to substantiate my feeling about his new way of life. I do have doubts, but we try very hard to overcome them because we love each other very much. Tommy has changed a lot from the time he began to communicate with us. he is much calmer and quieter than he used to be . His posture is more balanced and upright. He can make eye contact for a much longer period of time. he knows that I appreciate this and I feel that he makes a special effort at dinner time to look me in the eye. He also smiles more and many times it is while he make eye contact. The hardest part of our relationship now is getting ready for the time my parents won't be around. I am his only sibling, and I know that he is worried that I am not familiar with his needs and lifestyle. My parents are preparing for this in the best way they can, but it is still a big concern for us and affects our relationship. They have dedicated their lives toward making our family as normal as possible. I know that they love us both and want what is best for us. It must be quite a juggling act to let me live my life and also worry about Tommy's future.)

Church

My involvement with the church has been an up-hill climb. My first remembrance was my Mom leaving me with some people I didn't know. Everyone seemed to know what was going on except me. I was frightened and retreated into my autistic world. She would come and get me some time later. I do remember the sanctuary. It was beautiful and already I recognized it for peace and serenity. That is where I referred to as going earlier in my book. I must have been very young as I don't remember any formal setting, just children playing. I do remember being at church a lot with my parents when they led the youth group and other activities. I was let to wander as long as I didn't bother anyone or thing. If I disappeared out of sight, someone would look for me and bring me back. It was one of my favorite places to be. Even then I was aware of my guides. They would communicate with me and keep me out of trouble. I was quite comfortable with them.

Then we must have changed churches, and I remember spending a lot of time in this one. It was not as grand physically, but it still had the awesome feeling of a higher power. My guides just transferred with me. People seemed really happy there and there were a lot of activities going on. We seemed to be always there.

By this time children my age were having Sunday school. I certainly couldn't fit into this situation. I was let run or else a very nice lady, named Mrs. Brown, would hold me on her lap and sometimes rock me. I always loved to be rocked even when I was too big for it. Later on, one of my parents would take me outside and walk or take me home. Everyone seemed to accept me or at least tolerate me and I remember it as a happy experience. I felt holy even in my state. I remember hearing bits and pieces about the bible, God and the usual stories. I always would liked to have corrected them on some things but had no way to do it. I didn't have it altogether in my mind either, but knew some of what they said was wrong. At that point, none of these people thought I had a thought in my head. They just felt sorry for my parents, who had the misfortune to have birthed such a beautiful but empty individual. (I was beautiful too – My unbiased parents told me so.)

We moved to Connecticut when I was twelve. I was having a lot of problems by then and my religious training pretty much came to a halt. My parents stayed actively connected to the new church, but they took turns going and someone stayed home with me.

People think we are unaware of those happenings, but we aren't. Most of the time we aren't sure why they are taking place as we are unaware of our noises and mannerisms. We are aware that others don't tolerate something about us. Our make-up is such that we care, but we don't care that much either. Our caring revolves around not getting to do what we want and seeing those few who we do care about and being hurt by this. It is all perplexing to us. As I have now improved, I care a lot about those things. It can be very hurtful and sometimes I wonder if it is worth it. All the trade-offs are always in progress.

At one point, in this church, a man started a class with some others who had disabilities. It went only for a short time. Our disabilities were so varied it was impossible to do. In fact I think I whacked him a couple of times. All I know is we didn't attend for very long. Our disability is so hard to understand, it is difficult to integrate us with other disabled. Hopefully things are different now, and people are better educated on how to interact with us. I will always feel good about that man, Mr. Shultz, and Mrs. Brown, in the other church; at least they tried.

All this time I was receiving messages from guides. They kept me in touch with the universe. My spiritual growth was being shaped without my knowing. I was very comfortable with this world beyond. In this world I didn't have to deal with all the insults to my sensitive system. I spent more time there than here. The foundation was being laid for my special gifts. I am not sure when I became aware of them.

I didn't think much about anyone else until I started to FC. I cared about my family but even that was from an egocentric place. I always was able to get inside another person's mind but thought everyone did that. Since I have more information about energy, I think much of what I can do has an energy base. My guides opened my eyes to the universe and I could see the spiritual world. I can remember it being a scary experience at first. Then the more I experienced it, I loved it. It is so simplified once you understand it. You people here on earth make it so complicated. Human nature, as you call it, wants to change all the rules. No one wants to think they are to blame for anything. I guess it makes you feel better while you are here.

I won't go into my spiritual beliefs here, but they have been being formulated for a long time. My parents are letting me have my head in these matters. I appreciate that. I have had the privilege of talking to several persons who are considered very knowledgeable in this area. I am not absolutely sure of what they think of me, but, at least, they put up a good front at accepting my ideas on equal ground. They appear to be amazed at my introspect and knowledge.

I have always wanted to go to church again. My noises and anxiety when I get excited have prevented this. I have worked so hard at ridding myself of these nuisances. I have worked up to usually being able to sit through a two-hour conference now; I do have my days however. The subject matter has to be of interest to me, also. I find anything to do with religion or spirituality fascinating. Anything to do with that subject I seem to retain, besides being able to tap into the universe.

Not very long ago, my parents asked if I wanted to try to go to church with them. We had tried a couple of times a while ago and failed miserably. We hardly got inside the doors and I got so excited I started making noise and had to leave. Our church isn't the kind where they might think I just received the spirit of the Lord. Our church is more the kind where many might perceive I was getting the spirit of the devil.

I was quite thrilled to have another chance. I told them if it was a good day, I might try it with them. Then my work on noise prevention started to take place. I need to concentrate long before the big event and I mean long – days before. I practice in my mind. I try to construct the event the best I can. That is why I need to have as many details as you can give me in advance. Unexpected things that are not on my agenda really throw me. Things like people hugging me or getting in my face without advanced permission. That really threatens my security. My parents are very aware of this. One or the other stay very close to me when a situation presents itself that unknowing people might do this. I know people are trying to be nice and regular people perceive this as an acceptance gesture. Oh, how I wish I could do that, but I am not there yet.

Back to going to church – I was being given a second chance.

126

We talked the whole situation over at home ad-nauseam. It was decided no decision could be made in advance. We just had to be prepared when a good day came. It meant we had to get up early every Sunday morning when I was home. This was to get all my compulsive self-care things done as well as my parents getting ready, also. Believe me I can't skip a thing. If we did, I would be noisy and couldn't go anyway. They said not to worry even if we all got ready and I said no! I worried about it a lot. In fact, we did this a couple of times before I actually made it. This day I could feel good vibes. My Mom impressed on me, it must be zero noise. They both told me if I couldn't do that, it was OK to leave and not feel a failure. Then one of my parents would go and the other stay So there we were going into church, looking a little like Rain Man and his brother going into the casino, sort of dressed alike, Dad making sure I wasn't self conscious by not wearing a tie that Sunday. It really doesn't matter, I don't want a tie anyway. God could care less.

They made sure I got there in plenty of time. I like music, so they let me sit in the balcony by the organ. I lasted until the sermon and then could feel the inability to keep quiet coming on. I FC-ed to Dad I wanted to go, so we did. I felt good about it and it paved the way for the next time.

My Mom stayed for the whole service. When she came home, she said the lady Assistant Minister had stopped her and told her, she saw me leave. She asked my Mom if there was anything she could do to make it more comfortable for me. She said she was preaching soon and maybe she could prepare the crowd for my being there. She already knew of me, because both she and the minister had used some of my poetry in their sermons. My Mom said it was very considerate of her but she would have to get my permission. I was not about to have the members have to tolerate me. I said no, that I wanted to do it on my own. It was really nice of her to offer. She is a very special lady. Then I kicked my concentration on zero noise into high gear. I meditated and visualized to the best of my limited ability. Within two weeks I asked to try again. This time I made it through the whole service. I was really impressed with myself. My parents were thrilled with both my success as well as the acceptance of me by the congregation. I showed off my FC skill to a few. They seemed to be impressed but asked the usual questions, "He doesn't always look at the board when typing," "How can you (my parents) read what he types so fast?" First question – I can't stare at the board for that long a time (sensory issues). The answer to the next – practice, practice, practice! I was really proud of myself. I didn't want to stay that long after church, as I wanted to leave a good impression.

Since then, I go fairly regular. We still make up our minds the morning of church. It is a bother, because of traffic in the bathroom. Me and my confounded routines and Mom doing all the things that women do. They are good about it though. Most of the time I can carry it through. Occasionally, we get as far as the church and I can feel my noises coming on. They do not push me, but I know of all the effort they have put in to get me there. I feel bad about this. I have a goal to join the church, but I want to do it the right way, not with people pitying me. We will see how this plays out.

My Relationship with God and Man

The place I dwell is in my mind and not my body.
It is the place my soul occupies as I go from life to life.
It is important that I recognize this
because God expects much from it.

The soul is our guide and we must listen to it.
Our mind can justify anything we wish it to.
Our mind can be manipulated by others.
The soul is of our making, we must live through it.

It is not in our best interests
to pray only in a crisis.
Prayers are not worthy if they are not sincere.
Believe and not pretend for he knows all.

128

He is a loving God, who will welcome us with open arms.
His revelations of good can change our lives forever.
Be ready to answer his call.
Kindness and mercy are his by-words.

Our lives are in his hands and he will not drop us
unless by our own will we wiggle free.
Have confidence in his power for it is our salvation.
Our future is in his grasp.

Most people think God is a prude who wants us to suffer.
This is far from true; most suffering is of our own choosing.
His mission for us sometimes requires it,
but joy and happiness are his gifts to us.

Our life requires us to be of good will to others for their sake.
If you count the stars in your crown you are doomed.
The reason to do good must be for the good.
We will perish in self-righteousness if we are not careful.

Self-righteousness is the root of most problems of the world.
It conquers us all from time to time in our lives –
One big mistake that has divided the world.
Most of our religions feel they have the corner on God.

I pray every day that my mission for God be of his choosing.
That he will guide me in his way and lead me in others' needs.
In this way I will know what his desires are.
May his place in my heart be always open to him.

His truth shall rule the universe and keep it safe from evil.
The evil we encounter will be of our own choosing.
Take control of me, God, and make me your servant,
for I will lovingly serve you all of my life.

Tom Page
May 18, 1998

Time Concept

I would like to spend a little energy discussing the concept of time. It is these inanimate and nonconcrete things that really throw me. You can mark off a calendar and learn the clock settings but not be able to conceptualize them internally. This is a big problem for me. Think of all the words you use in the language that pertain to it such as before, after, soon, later, not now, in a little bit, you only have a minute, you have a little time yet, tomorrow, last night, etc. Time put in that context is meaningless to me and a lot of other persons with autism. How long is later anyway? I have enough problems with processing and language and then add something abstract and it just doesn't get through. Top it off with difficulties in generalizing. This causes me always to worry about being late as I don't have a clue if we are or not. All I know is that it seems to be very important in life. Sometimes it makes me frantic when we get someplace, because I don't know if I'm early or late. Other times I don't hurry for the same reason. Sometimes it helps to tell me we are right on time. The key word is sometimes as I'm not very predictable in this area yet.

If you can't conceptualize time, you don't know where you are in hours, days or years. Therefore, you must make your own markers. Many of us do it by routines. There are certain things that happen everyday like eating meals, showering, and things in between. I use those for my basic markers. Then fill in things that happen often. . That is one reason many of us cling so to our routines. When they are disrupted, we have no idea where we are time wise in the day. They must get back on track to proceed. This is a very big problem for me. I have been known to sit up all night because my evening routine was disrupted. I really know how long a night can be. That is when I long to have a person with me that can FC and understand me. People thought they were doing something good for me by taking me some place special, like a concert. They were and I truly wanted to go. My good time was spoiled as I was so anxious to get back into my routine and time frames. When I get home I want to go back to the time place where my routine was disrupted and quickly go through the steps that I missed. They don't have to be elaborate, just there. Then I can proceed with the rest of the night in comfort. That is why it is so important to have someone with me who understands me at this point in my life. I know this sounds strange to everyone, even me, but that is the way it is. I'm trying to get better at this problem because it is ruining my life. I can't expect everybody to understand my idiosyncrasies, but I can't yet develop the time concepts to do things the way you do. I am trying to just forget about my inability to conceptualize and do things the way you do. Sometimes though, autism just takes over. This makes me inflexible and difficult to understand. I hope God will provide me with people who can get into my head or at least until I can defeat this demon. I want to state that this is my own personal problem and not all persons with autism have this in such a severe form. They have their demons, I have mine.

ELUSIVE TIME

One elusive mystery is time.
To capture its meaning would be sublime.
It seems to make the world go round,
If a way to understand it could be found.

The terms now and today never stay still,
Sooner or later are words used at your will.
Yesterday and tomorrow are never quite clear,
Few words of this nature are ever really here.

How much is more, how little is less,
All of this talk gets my head in a mess.
In a little while, how long is that?
These phrases to you seem quite pat.

Our minds don't work like that, I'm afraid.
A much better foundation needs to be laid.
Linked to an event we all know,
Such as, after dinner we will go.

—*Tom Page, 1997*

Dad Feels Tom's Persistence and FC Helped Save His Life

It was about the time that Dad and I got good at FC that I began to see a change in his aura. For those of you that don't understand, it is a glow I can see around some people. It is an indicator of both their mental and physical health. I only get concerned when there is a drastic change from their usual image. I don't use it often but it is like a barometer to a weather man. It doesn't tell the weather but gives indications of changes to come.

Dad's aura wasn't right and was getting worse. We would FC every day and one day I told him I wish he would go to the doctor. He said he had been to his heart doctor and urologist not very long ago. I told him it was important that he go now. Dad dismissed it and we went on to something else. I knew he didn't believe me so I waited until the next day and tried again. He was nice, but he reminded me again of his visits. We did this for about a week, and then he told me he had his annual physical in a couple of months and would be OK. I still told him it was important he go now, but he dismissed it.

Soon Mommy got in on it, but she was no help to me, neither of them understood about auras. I just kept at it until we had a session with Sue, our energy therapist. She understands about auras and explained the importance of the color. That put a new spin on it. Every time Dad and I FC-ed I still begged him to go to the doctor. He and Mom talked it over and decided he should go. He made up a sickness excuse to get into the doctor. When he went in, he explained to the doctor that I was worried about him and wanted the doctor to examine him. The doctor looked him over but found nothing wrong. He made the following remark to Dad, "I'll let you know when I buy a new car and you can let him pick it out for me." Dad let it pass but was annoyed.

As Dad was leaving the office he ask the doctor if he had received the blood report the urologist had ordered. The doctor looked in his folder and saw that Dad had a substantial increase in his PSI score.

(Dad – There was some kind of misunderstanding between the blood laboratory, my doctor and my urologist because my urologist did not get the report. Thank goodness Tom had pushed hard for the visit to the doctor's office). His urologist was notified and took over. He had a series of tests performed and found cancer. Thank God we found it in time. It had not spread and was treated with radiation. It has not come back and Dad feels it was my persistence that helped save his life. I feel God saved his life through me. I prayed for help many times.

I know that Dad and Mom both feel that this story is the best proof that anyone could have that our FC is real. We have not told this story around to many people because the skeptics who don't believe would love to discredit it so others would not believe.

Moved to a Group Home

I have touched on the subject of my move to the group home. I would like to go into it more. Remember, at this time my parents didn't have any idea of my understanding of what went on in the world. I hadn't really put it together very well either. All I had in my head were lots of separate facts and intense loosely bound feelings. I was like a loose cannon with no one aiming or properly loading and firing. I was just there and most people stayed clear of the often combustible, misfiring object. I was twenty-six and my parents were naturally worried about my and their future. No one in our state was taking autistic adults into residential settings. There was lots of talk about this subject in our house. I wasn't sure what that all meant. I just knew it had to do with my leaving. The only leaving I knew about was my Grandmother's death and Sally's going to college. Grandma never came back and Sally came and left mysteriously all the time. I didn't think I had anything to do with Grandma, but I sure thought I did with Sally. Both events caused tears and unhappiness. So when I heard bits and pieces about me, I didn't exactly associate it with pleasure. I could feel much anxiety from my parents whenever the subject came up.

They started having meetings, sometimes at our house, with other anxiety ridden parents. I was always lying on the sofa, my usual spot, in the family room. I was as addicted to it as my chair in the old work-place. In fact, I still am most of the time, **now**. Even though they met in our living room, I could hear them very well. I don't ever remember them discussing any of it with me directly. So, I just worried. All of this went on and on.

My parents seemed to be taking the lead in this. I interpreted this to mean they really wanted me out of the house. We spent a lot of time going around in the car looking at houses for sale. They thumbed them up and down with their talk. I assumed they were moving me into one of them, but no one ever asked me how I felt about anything – there were more Meetings-Meetings-waiting-waiting. I was quite depressed by that time, and my behavior followed suit. They weren't in a terrific mood themselves.

My Mom stopped going to her job at the school I attended. She worked on this project at home a lot. I don't think she was very enthused about heading this up. Her not being at school was another change I didn't need. She still did most of my transportation, pillows and all.

(Mom – The decisions and changes in our lives (deciding to start Opportunity House) did not come about easily. I was very wary of taking on this responsibility. As I have often said, I went into it feeling somewhat pushed. (kicking and screaming all the way). Then it became an obsession and was discussed constantly in our house. I'm sure our daughter felt a change, and not particularly a good one for her. This started happening when we moved to CT. It must have been difficult for her. It was done for all our survival and we all hope for a satisfactory conclusion).

One day reality set in and they decided on a place. They must have talked to me about things as they happened, but I don't remember it. Mostly, it was to each other or other concerned people. In fact they talked of little else. Sally was gone from our house by this time. Either married or about to be, I think.

We started making regular visits to the new place. I had no idea what was happening, just not good feelings about it. After awhile we started changing the place. I was included when they did painting and other construction work there. Not only me, but there were other students from my school, with their parents, also. We persons with autism just wandered around, some getting into trouble, but all of us needing watching. I remember one night everybody getting excited when one person with autism nearly set the house on fire. It caused them to rethink the stove in the kitchen. I knew the other persons, somewhat, who later became the residents of my group home. Compatibility didn't seem to be on anybody's mind, then. If so, not many of us would have chosen each other for roommates. All but one came directly from their home. We later became tolerable as "roomies." It was a rough beginning for everybody, including the staff. I don't think any one of us had any idea about what was going on. We were used to being herded around like cattle. When it got too bad or insulted our senses most of us could certainly act out behaviorally.

People talk about persons with autism beings friends with each other. I've heard parents and staff say so and so are good friends. I'm not sure most people with autism understand what that means since we have so many problems with relationships. We certainly care what happens to each other and worry about it but I am not sure why. It doesn't seem to fit your definition of a friend. I think we try to mimic your actions as it seems to please you. I know you want us to have this experience as you think it will make us happy as it does you. We are not made up like you, however. We long to go places and do things like you, but I am not sure it is the same for most of us. We would much rather be "friends" with someone we can trust to help us out in situations we can't handle like parents, staff, etc. It can be nice or not nice to have others like ourselves along. It just depends upon the situation. I am just speaking for myself here.

Back to the move to the home. We future residents watched as furniture was moved in, the lawn was mowed, even flowers were planted. My Mom and Dad worked at home talking everything over with each other with me listening and wondering in the background. I do remember them talking to me at some point. They were telling me things like, I was old enough to leave home like Sally had done.

I didn't even understand why she had left. They said I would like where I was going to live. They told me I would see them everyday. They made sure I saw where I was going to sleep. They said all this in the most positive way, but their eyes and vibes said just the opposite. I was terrified and could tell they were, too. Why were they doing this?

I was still going to my old work program. Evidently, they were taking in the new residents a few at a time. My Mom would be at the group home all day, then pick me up at the workplace, take me home to Dad, then go back to the group home for many long nights. I was the last one to make the dreaded entrance. I found out later, they weren't planning on putting me in this first home at all. It was a last-minute decision, as most of the parents involved with the planning, didn't want to be the guinea pigs. Everyone wanted their person in the planned second home with all the problems solved. Anyway my parents decided to take the plunge in case the second home didn't materialize. That was a real vote of confidence for me. They weren't even sure this would fly.

The last week before I moved out tensions were mounting. Piles of underwear, socks and PJ's were making stacks on the floor. I could see Mom crying silently every once in awhile. Dad was grouchy. This all made me really confident to go to my future home. Why were we doing this? Regardless of my feelings, everything kept progressing.

Finally the day came when all of my new and a lot of my old things were moved. I was asked to participate in carrying these things into my new bedroom. There was another person that I was to share the room with. I had seen him around my work place, but he was not very familiar to me. I didn't much like his looks and I don't think he liked mine. No one asked either of us if we wanted to be together. My new bed wasn't there yet and they put a rollaway in for me to sleep on.

When I came to my real home from my work place, we all got in the car to go to my new home. My parents were full of vibes. They kept smiling and telling me how wonderful it would be. Not for an instant did they fool me. I was most unhappy! They were too! They hung around for a long time and tried to instruct the staff to every detail of my care. They were worried I might hurt them and me physically. The staff didn't really know my potential even though they had been told. The first of many battles came that night when they tried to put me through my bedtime routine. I know I tried to hit some of them and push them around. Finally, they got me in that flimsy bed. I don't remember if I slept or not, I was so scared! The next morning I was trying to do what they wanted me to do in self-care. They sure didn't understand my problems and I sure didn't understand them. It ended up with me chasing them all over the place and landing a hit when ever I could catch one. The guy in charge hid behind the sofa. This gave me a feeling of power. Bad thing! I became a bully. A scared bully who wanted to go home. My parents spent as many hours there as they did at their own home. More, probably. We stuck it out though things didn't improve much. The poor staff – I was one of three who were potentially difficult in the behavioral sense. It was a three-ring circus. Someone was having a problem most of the time. Although I wanted to leave, I can't say it wasn't interesting. A show most of the time! It kept you on your toes as you never knew when you might become part of it.

I wonder what it would be like now. This was long ago when not much help was available, besides medication. Even that was trial and error. A lot of behavior modification was tried with limited success. A lot of time-out rooms were common, and I certainly did time in there. I really welcomed them as I had little control over my behavior after it got to the point of no return. Even though I was a bully, I felt a great deal of remorse when I calmed down. I could see the hurt and frustration in my parents' eyes. I cared about them so much. I cared very little about the staff and I imagine the feeling was mutual. The ones that stayed, I wonder why. Things did improve but it took a long time.

I still live there. I still would rather live at home, but I have reconciled my feelings about the situation. Since I now can express myself, things have changed dramatically. I have a lot of say in my life now. I go places and see many things. Most of staff respect me. Some can talk to me. My parents are still very much involved with me. We are making plans for me to live in a smaller unit. I will have a lot of say in this one. I still fear all of this will be taken away.

Staff come and go. A few stay for a variety of reasons. Some stay because they truly like their job and really get into us. They are few, sad to say. Many are caught up in their own personal problems, and we are either a stability factor or they lack the motivation to move on. We are in the position of having to adjust to each one. Few are good in every area. Some are really caring and make our life interesting but can't get it together enough to make sure we have hat and gloves when needed. Some are very task oriented and always make sure we have hat and gloves, but don't understand us as persons at all. We are, indeed, hard to understand but not impossible if you truly take the time and truly care enough. We tend to latch on to the few who can do this with us as individuals. We become dependent on them, then live with the fright they will leave and many of them do. I think some of the persons with autism are so afraid of getting hurt, they won't take the chance and become known as not being able to develop relationships. It is devastating to have a staff friend who promises to carry on some sort of relationship when they leave, only never to hear from them again or maintain a "sort of" relationship for a short time that peters out. When that happens, you are afraid to try again. It is good to have a staff friend who is really in to you personally. I'm used to it by now.

Energy/FC

I want to explore the whole realm of energy and how it interfaces with FC. I know this is a controversial subject. Everyone knows energy has a scientific basis and everyone knows everything is made up of energy-producing molecules. Energy changes constantly. Energy is prevalent in relationships. Vibrations are really energy. It could be said that intuition is also a form of energy. It is all around us. Energy comes in many different forms.

Energy is essential in FC. It makes a difference in the way the words come through. It is different each time two people facilitate.

When energy is distributed correctly between the facilitator and the user, ideas and words come out in a productive manner. Many times the energy is counterproductive. One or both people are out of sync energy wise. There is a big difference between positive and negative energies. If there is enough negative energy around, it can stop the process completely. That is where expectations are important. Good expectations produce positive energy. It is a little like magnets and batteries with their polar points. If the correct ends are put together you get results. If the opposing ends are put together you get resistance. It actually pushes energy apart. If the magnet is too strong for the counterpart, even if the correct ends are together, it will not be the proper balance that leads to correct messages. The same is true with partners in FC. Proper balance leads to proper messages. When the facilitator has too much energy for the user, the above happens. Our thoughts are clouded and we get carried away in their energy state. We are not sure if it is our thoughts or theirs. It is evident sometimes when the FC output becomes very rapid and seems to fly off the board. It is a euphoric state and very pleasurable, like a drug. One loves this state but afterwards we become scared and have no way to stop the process. I didn't understand the difference until I begin to separate self from non-self. It is no one's fault as it usually happens slowly and builds. The facilitator thinks it is going well. Then both parties get excited and the energies get out of control. These facilitators are usually some of the best. Their channels are wide open and available to the user. It is only once in a while they are too open and our energies are too strongly flowing together. They are some of our favorite people and we don't want to lose them. A grounding agent has to be there. People with autism have little of this quality. Therefore, the facilitator must accept most of the responsibility. Some people have this grounding ability naturally, but a few fly without a tail. I'm not sure how you obtain a tail, but maybe Sue, or someone like her, could help. Most people with autism I know have not separated themselves from others. Therefore, they are more vulnerable to this infusion of energies. Don't interpret this to mean that they don't have ideas or what they say isn't their own. It just means they can be more susceptible to energy flows.

I am just beginning to separate my energy from one who is overpowering in energy flow. I can't always do it but I am starting to recognize when it is getting out of control and try to maintain my independence. Sometimes it works and sometimes it doesn't.

The opposite can also be true. The facilitator can also produce so little energy that there is nothing to relate to. It is like a wimpy handshake. Nothing there that you care to establish ties with. It is important that both parties hold up their part. There are many reasons why people can't FC with each other. The energy between them is the biggest obstacle to overcome. Fear, doubt, being uncomfortable with the situation as well as a noncommitment attitude are all a part of energy nonproductiveness.

Energy is not as mystifying as you think. The English language is full of references to it. Have you ever been in a room where two people are getting angry with each other? It feels like the room is getting warmer. It truly is, as energy molecules are moving faster. Ever heard of the term hot and bothered? What do you think that refers to? Have you ever heard of a person referred to as cold or frigid, or as a situation between two people as cool? Words as charisma and sex appeal are thought to be mystifying as well. They are really forms of energy that most people find positive. Taking all this into consideration, no wonder testing in court cases doesn't work! I rest my case – enough said!

The world knows a great deal about external energy but very little about internal energy.

Coping on Vacations

My family had always taken vacations with me included. Most of the time they were super, but occasionally there were moments of disaster. Like I said before, it was not often but enough to always have a note of tension riding with us. When I was little it was not a big problem. They could always pass it off as little boy tantrums, he needs a nap, etc.. How big can you get before this begins to look ridiculous. Pretty big in my case as I was always big for my age. It would be embarrassing for us at the time, but my parents would usually get a sense of humor about it after awhile. They would talk about the funny parts or make jokes about the situation. I'm sure there was a dark side that they tried to hide from me. I would see Mom cry sometimes. In those days there was no one to turn to for help. There were times when I got older and bigger, they would really get frustrated and yell at me and tell me off good and proper. Interestingly, when I was in this condition, I had no control over my senses. They would cut on and off in an irrational pattern, but I could really feel my parents' anger. That would really make things worse and I would be more hard to handle. This type of situation turns into a round robin where neither party can help their actions. One perpetuates the other and becomes a self-fulfilling prophecy. Anyway, we traveled all over the U.S.A.

Fun Trip to Daytona

One of our favorite places to go was to Daytona Beach, Florida. I loved the water and could handle myself in it very well. When I was about five I could jump off the high dive, and my head would not go under the water when I entered it. My parents said the other kids called me "cork head." I soon learned to manipulate the waves. It was easy for me. I loved feeling the power of water. My body instinctively did all the right things. When others much larger than me were running from the waves, I was heading out for the big ones. It was a good thing my family could handle themselves in the ocean as they spent a lot of time chasing me. They knew I loved it so much and soon they were making yearly trips there. My pattern was set into a daily routine. Wake up, go to the ocean, then to the pool till lunch, lay down take a nap, up again, out to the ocean, then pool, shower, go to the boardwalk with rides, back to the motel, maybe take a walk on the beach or sit on the balcony where I could listen to the ocean and view the pool. Dad and I would go to a restaurant and get some toast, then to bed. I was happy as a clam if we kept my schedule. We would end the vacation brown and water wrinkled. This became an annual event and frankly I wasn't as enthusiastic, but no one knew and we just kept going. I wasn't unhappy about it, but it might not have been my choice if I had a voice. My parents thought they were giving me my ultimate pleasure.

The Magic Kingdom Turned Ugly

During the vacation each year, we used to make a one-day trip to Disney World. We would always return to the motel at Daytona Beach the same night. I loved it! I also remembered where all the rides were in the Magic Kingdom. One year we were with my sister and her family in Florida. I was a grown person by then. My folks were going to give us all an extra treat and stay one night at one of the expensive hotels at Disney World. Well guess what, that threw Tom a curve. When we checked in, I became worried. It was different than our usual routine. When we went to the Magic Kingdom, I was anxious and edgy. Then when we went back to the hotel, I was a wreck. No one told me we were not going back to the motel at Daytona Beach as we usually did. I remember going from the Magic Kingdom in a boat to a fancy motel. I also remember my parents had me between them and me yelling intermittently and generally being obnoxious. Long boat trip! I didn't sleep until early in the morning so none us, Mom, Dad and I, got any sleep. Thank heavens, Sally and her family were on their own that night. I was fine the next day, tired but fine. We were all tired. My parents didn't figure out that the problem was communication until years later. At that time most of our communication was by instinct, which wasn't too bad.

Turn to God AND Listen

My reason to write this new story is to show that training and the recognition of God's power does pay off. I was involved in an auto accident last week while my parents were on vacation and not even in the country to come to my aid. It was a terrifying experience. My driver pulled out in front of a truck. It hit us broadside. There was lots of damage to our car. I was sitting in the front passenger's seat. When the car stopped I was sitting with glass all over me and a sore body but no blood. My fellow passengers were panicky as they should be. An important part of my new life is faith in God. It is a routine habit to turn to God for help in a crisis. I could feel his presence and guidance to meditate and pray for all concerned. It gave me a feeling of peace and confidence. When help arrived I was very fortunate that the staff member from my work place was a calm and confident person. He helped me get into the ambulance and go the emergency room. This would have been impossible a few years ago. Lying down and getting into a strange vehicle with flashing lights is not my cup of tea. When we got to the hospital I was taken to the emergency room. I felt calm during my whole experience there. It lasted about six hours. During the whole time I was ask to lay on my back and stomach for special tests. I DON'T think I could have done it without my special sensory training where I am asked to do many things in several positions. I am also used to laying on my back for energy therapy. After we were in the emergency for awhile, we switched staff members. She was also calm and reassuring. Can you imagine TOM Page going through six hours of things such as ambulance ride, MRI, Cat Scan and orders from people I didn't know.

I LIKE THE NEW TOM!

PART 5
Other Samples of My Writings

How I Started Writing

In the interest of the reader I want you to know that I wanted to write before I could FC. I would sit and watch others do things and became an observer of humanity. As Dad would say I'm a people watcher. I wanted to write stories like the ones I had read in past lives. The lives of people are interesting and the world is, too. The people that can record it become shapers as well as recorders. I want to become a shaper and recorder, also. I want my writing to be what I call worthy of the reader and humanity. Entertainment but with a message. I was not aware I would get the opportunity with FC. It was when I wrote my first poem with Mom that a whole new world opened up for me. People liked it and I was off the starting blocks and still in the race.

We used to get bulletins about FC from both Maine and the Syracuse group. Included were works from FC users. They were sometimes primitive and sometimes sophisticated. Also there was poetry from some users. Mom read them to me and I was fascinated. She ask me if I thought I could do something like that.

It was as if a light bulb went on in my head. Maybe I really would get a chance to express myself through words. The first time we sat down and tried, it was successful. I spent a lot of time, and I do have a lot of time, sitting around thinking of what I might write about. I wanted to do it every chance I got. We produced and to this day I still like most of what I wrote. The poetry I produced then was mostly about the frustrations of my autism. It has been expanded along with my other areas of growth. In fact it is a good barometer of my improvement. I don't get a chance to do it as much, with my other writings. I do love to do it and want to get back to it some day.

Now, I want to tell you about an incident that shaped my writing opportunities with Dad. We were attending a conference on FC at Syracuse University and went to a small session on poetry writing. They had about eight to ten persons with autism sitting in a semi-circle, each with a facilitator. The leader explained that we were going to write a poem together. He had a person with autism, who was with him, start it off. Then each of us were to add a verse until it was done. I did not know when I took my seat I would be the first one in line to add a verse. To make matters worse Mom had to leave for a while and that left Dad as my facilitator. We were just getting to the point where he was feeling comfortable facilitating with me. All of a sudden here we were in full view of a room full of strangers and having to FC poetry on a subject we just heard of. Dad panicked and would have left if he could have gracefully. We both bit the bullet and started to FC. God must have known we needed special help because the words came easy and people liked what they heard. From that day on we have enjoyed many conferences. We all need to stick with it until the day we get over the hump. It is just like the sled ride. Climbing a snowy hill is tough, but what a wonderful ride down. Sometimes the hill is extra steep, but that makes the ride all the better.

It was story writing I first tried with Dad. It was because he and I had been reading several books about the early history of our country that I chose to write about a wagon-train master. It is an interesting profession and requires a lot of leadership qualities that a person must have to successfully handle a crew of his own plus a list of families that he has not known. Add all that to a journey through many different kinds of possible disasters and you have material unlimited. I decided during the writing of it to make it a training book for leadership by making each chapter require a different technique to handle the problems. I wrote about ten chapters and set it aside for awhile until I can develop my writing skills a little more. I love the story and want to do a better job.

While doing the story I thought about many things that I felt were important in life. When you are autistic, like I am, you have many hours to think about life. When Dad would meet with me in the evening I would write down a thought I had in mind. It really was a thrill to see his reaction. He never knew I had a deep understanding of life before. We showed them to Mom, who was surprised too, but knew there was something under my hat besides a head of hair to fill up the space and only be a carpet for an empty room. Dad and Mom showed the thoughts to a few of their close friends and professionals. All were astounded, so we decided to send a dozen each of these thoughts to close friends for Christmas. We called the packet "The Thought of the Month." We sent the packet as a Christmas present to close friends who believed in me. It was thrilling to hear their response. I want to publish them someday.

A friend of mine from Maine asked me if I would like make a presentation at a conference, with two other people that have autism. It was my first chance to tell others how I felt about autism. After our speeches were read, we fielded questions from the audience. Thank goodness Mom was beside me with her positive vibes.

That is something important to understand: we need positive energy with us to do our best.

A short time later I was asked again to give a presentation with another person with autism. This time it was on spirituality, and Laurie was the facilitator We used the same format that we used before. I now feel confident writing a speech and fielding questions after it is read. I have been lucky; I have been asked to present at more conferences.

It seems as though if you can FC with me, you should be able to write poetry and stories with me. The answer is, not really! No one wishes this to happen more than me. The truth is it takes a special relationship with me as well as we being able to FC. Again the dynamics are different. Most people choke even when trying to create for themselves. There comes the old bug-a-boo-pressure and negative energy. The relationship changes. Our fragile systems can not get through the barrier. I have only been able to be productive with five or six people. I hope this changes soon.

I have inserted samples of my work throughout this book so you can see what I enjoy doing. Two more poems and five thoughts are added on the following pages. I hope this is just the beginning of many writings as I have much I want to say.

This was my first Annual Christmas Poem.

Good Will To Men,
Then Peace On Earth

On this great earth
God gave us diversity
and the ability to pick and chose.

He also made the inhabitants
in an array of colors, abilities
and individual preferences.

Man also came with a nature
subject to ego and love of power.
Since the creation of time
this has caused friction
which has never been resolved.

This is the time of the year to reflect
on what **Good Will to Men**
really means.
When we truly solve this conflict
only then can we have everlasting
Peace on Earth

Tom Page
December 14, 1997

This was to my Mother on Mother's Day.

Past, Present and Future Love

I love you today and forever.
I will love you as others never have.
My love is everlasting
and is the past, present and future.

I give it freely with no strings attached.
It is not for sale.
It is powerful and steadfast
in its potential to hold the world in its grasp.

It is like a passion that is in its infancy
and like a plant that continues to grow,
it will never stop.
It is like an unbridled colt in its growing stage,
either too little control or too immense
an amount.

It will never end in this world
but go on through eternity.

— Tom Page

It Is The Desire To Understand All People and Respect Their Ability That Makes A Great Man

The men who knew their business best are the ones that were willing to get their hands dirty. The dirty hands is not a sign of low level activity but sign of getting to the job and sometimes show your ignorance. A man is not looked down on because he is not understanding of everything but only for acting like he does and really doesn't. Only when he will ask questions and listens to answers and be willing to participate will he gain true respect and knowledge. Lincoln is a prime example he learned this from people because they knew he was sincere and would take instruction and give them credit. He learned farming, store keeping, and the law. His political life came from caring about people. It must be a wonderful feeling to rise to the top with the help of so many people, who gave of themselves because you were worthy or their assistance. I guess dirty hands does't say it right. The ability to be sophisticated enough to listen to a farmer, a store clerk, a lawyer and even the lowly workman on the riverboat barges to New Orleans. He would not approve of that word lowly because he knew it is a term of arrogance used by people who did not understand and respect their fellowman.

— Tom Page

Responsibility Is Part Of Power and Real People Must Accept It

In the time we are now, we should not be a person who does his thing and lets others do theirs. The world is small and our thing has a profound affect on all others. It is our responsibility to take others into consideration when doing our thing. The Lord gave us power to be special and he expects us to use it responsibly and our power will grow.

— Tom Page 1998

It Is The Act That Counts
Not The Size Of It

In this world we are but a drop in the bucket.
The time we spend is very minute. It makes us
very humble indeed when we look at it this way.
We must take a different perspective. If we make
a sound today, it will still be heard for millions of
years across the universe. If we make a motion it
can be seen in the same way. We may not be aware
of it but life is one big camcorder. Scientist hope
some day to hear and see many events of the past.
We may find that some of our most insignificant
acts may have had a profound effect on life, and
some of our most memorable events we staged
have had little. God said it is not the size of a
seed that is important but what it grows.

— Tom Page 1998

The Relationship of Man To Man

In my opinion we can save the world if we can get outside ourselves and feel for our fellowman. He is our brother good or bad and we must extend a helping hand. We can not do it for him but we must pattern ourselves after God and be there when he is ready for us to save him. This is our little bit that makes a mountain when joined with others. Mountains make worlds and worlds make the universe.

Tomorrow Is Too Late
To Love Your Enemies

It is a great world when you are on top, but when you aren't the world is a crummy place. That is the perspective of the American people in these times. They have but one view point, they must be #1. It will be their downfall. Nobody is #1 in heaven, so Americans stay away or you will be miserable. I know I am being sarcastic but think about it. The world does not exist for living souls to compete. It is here for all to share. It is not the person considered on top that God really cares about, but the one who contributes to all people's happiness. Be careful how you interpret that. It gives a person a lot of responsibility. It must include all, even your enemies. Their welfare becomes important for true happiness. It is a world that cares which is world of peace. True caring is a powerful tool that can penetrate thick armor. It has been successful in this world since time began. Words are important but the unspoken language is the true communication. Some of us call it vibrations, but it is what you send that others feel. The interesting thing is that sometimes your friend is your enemy. He is not an open rival but hopes you will stumble. He is the dangerous one. He will be so easy to hate because he did you wrong. That is the true test, can you love him anyway.

— Tom Page 1999

Smiles came easy then . .

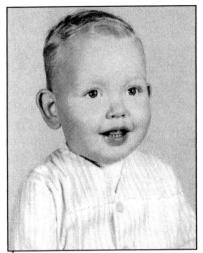

First professional picture

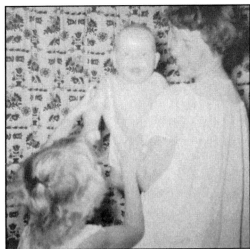

They were proud of me

I loved motion

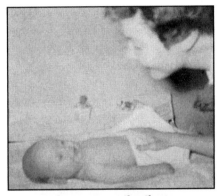

It was connecting time

I was an early climber

Must have been funny

Loved that water . . .

Water felt great coming down

It was't cold to me, just fun

Let go Mom, I want to swim

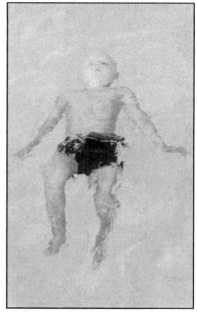

It worked, I'm swimming at age three

Growing up . . .

It is one of my favorite things

I was probably being tickled

Part of my therapy

Smiles on demand, hard to come by

The family . . .

Sally's husband took the picture

I said I was an uncle

I'm welcomed now, not just tolerated. Photo taken at my parents' retirement party